"A Noble Unrest"

"A Noble Unrest"
Contemporary Essays on the Work of George MacDonald

Edited by

Jean Webb

CAMBRIDGE SCHOLARS PUBLISHING

"A Noble Unrest": Contemporary Essays on the Work of George MacDonald, edited by Jean Webb

This book first published 2007 by

Cambridge Scholars Publishing

15 Angerton Gardens, Newcastle, NE5 2JA, UK

British Library Cataloguing in Publication Data
A catalogue record for this book is available from the British Library

Copyright © 2007 by Jean Webb and contributors

All rights for this book reserved. No part of this book may be reproduced, stored in a retrieval system, or transmitted, in any form or by any means, electronic, mechanical, photocopying, recording or otherwise, without the prior permission of the copyright owner.
ISBN 1-84718-154-6; ISBN 13: 9781847181541

... repose is not the end of education; its end is a noble unrest, an ever renewed awaking from the dead a ceaseless questioning of the past for the interpretation of the future ...

—George MacDonald, *A Dish of Orts* – "The Imagination: Its Functions and Culture", 1867.

TABLE OF CONTENTS

Introduction 1

Chapter One 6
George MacDonald and Social Issues
David Neuhouser

Chapter Two...15
Realism, Fantasy and a Critique of Nineteenth Century Society in George MacDonald's *At the Back of the North Wind*
Jean Webb

Chapter Three...33
"A Sort of a Fairy Tale": Narrative and Genre in George MacDonald's *Little Daylight*
Rachel Johnson

Chapter Four 44
Differences and Similarities: *Little Daylight* and *The Light Princess*
Yuko Ashitagawa

Chapter Five...59
Natural History—The Heavenly Sort: MacDonald's Integration of Faith and Reason, Religion and Science
Larry Fink

Chapter Six...67
MacDonald and Pullman, or: (Great-great-) Grandfather George
Bill Gray

Chapter Seven 84
Voice, Gender and Alterity in George MacDonald's Fairy Tales
Maria Nikolajeva

Chapter Eight 104
Journeys Into Darkness: Joseph Conrad's *Heart of Darkness* and George MacDonald's *Lilith*
Elmar Schenkel

Chapter Nine 122
Liminality as Psychic Stage in MacDonald's *Lilith*
Roderick McGillis

Chapter Ten 131
George MacDonald in the Creative Writing Classroom: "The Wise Woman as a Possible Model"
Thom Saterlee

Chapter Eleven 137
Story and the Child Reader Today
Judith Elkin

Contributors 150

INTRODUCTION

JEAN WEBB

The Scottish author George MacDonald (1824-1905) was a major nineteenth century writer, notably of fairy tales and works of fantasy, predominantly for children. W.H. Auden, C.S. Lewis, and G.K. Chesterton amongst others, cite MacDonald as a writer who changed their perceptions and influenced their work. His work was strongly influenced by his Christian beliefs, Romanticism and his own theories of the imagination. MacDonald's work falls into the period of children's literature known as the Golden Age of Fantasy, being grouped with Charles Kingsley, Lewis Carroll and Edward Lear as pushing the boundaries of the imagination and taking writing in English into new worlds and explorations of the self and society. MacDonald's fiction, whilst categorised as fantasy, also writes into the realities of the social context, critiquing the philosophical and moral tenets of the Victorian period. Fantasy and realism are often combined in his fiction, as in *At the Back of the North Wind*, producing a view of Victorian society which crosses class boundaries, giving the contemporary reader insights into the effects of growing industrialism and capitalism. The work incorporates debates of the period, such as Darwinism versus spirituality; humanity versus the growing pressures of Utilitarianism. His fairy tales have a spiritual quality and an other-worldliness. MacDonald interrogated the qualities of humanity and notions of the psyche, akin to A.E. Hoffman, and thereby moved English literature for children closer to the fantastic rather than the more "comfortable" fantasy of later writers such as Kenneth Grahame and A.A. Milne who created Arcadian worlds for children. MacDonald was also writing at a time of high consciousness of imperialism and colonialism, as typified, for example, by the work of G.A. Henty, the prolific writer of boy's adventure stories of Empire. The innovative early Modernist narrative style and form employed by MacDonald, emphasises the reader, thus moving away from the dominance of the omniscient narrator. He thereby produced texts which raise questions and stimulate the imagination and intellect of the reader both Victorian and contemporary.

MacDonald's body of work therefore raises interesting and important areas of consideration which are as pertinent today as in the Victorian era, such as the inter-connection between fantasy and realism; the conceptualisation of the imagination and how this is translated into literary expression; reflection upon questions of spirituality and morality; the construction of the hero and gender; consideration of fairy tale and readership; the inter-relationship between MacDonald's writing and adult Modernist writers, for example Joseph Conrad author of the iconic novel *Heart of Darkness*, and the relevance of MacDonald's work for the teaching of contemporary creative writing.

This collection of essays by invited academics of international standing, and lesser known new critical writers, explores and interrogates these positions and questions presenting a valuable contribution to the fields of the study of nineteenth and twentieth century literature; children's literature; genre studies and cultural studies. Most of the essays were presented as papers at "The George MacDonald Centenary Conference" held at the University of Worcester, UK in July, 2005. Others have been specially invited to contribute to produce a very strong representation of contemporary critical writing and approaches to literary studies focussing on the work of George MacDonald from their various perspectives.

The essays have been organised as a chronological critical consideration of aspects of George MacDonald's work from the social context in the nineteenth century, to critical readings employing contemporary literary theory, to the pertinence of MacDonald today both for potential creative writers and for young readers. David Neuhouser's essay, "George MacDonald and Social Issues" sets a social context placing MacDonald as being aware of social issues such as poverty, the role of women, environmental concerns, and animal rights. MacDonald, was, for example influenced by John Kennedy, who raised his awareness to social concerns and F.D. Maurice, who advocated Christian Socialism and the responsibility of the individual. Neuhouser demonstrates such awareness in MacDonald's novels and also how such concerns were addressed in MacDonald's work in the everyday world. As with other nineteenth century writers and thinkers such as John Ruskin, it is pertinent to note the inter-relationship between MacDonald's social philosophy and the development of the Welfare State in Britain, and pressing contemporary global issues such as preservation of the environment.

Jean Webb's "Realism, Fantasy and a Critique of Nineteenth Century Society in George MacDonald's *At the Back of the North Wind*" is a close textual analysis which examines MacDonald's theories of the imagination in relation to his novel, whilst demonstrating links between *At the Back of the North Wind* and the genre of the realist social problem novel written for adults. "A Sort of a Fairy Tale: Narrative and Genre in George MacDonald's *Little Daylight*" by Rachel Johnson, continues the development of the overall discussion with a detailed consideration of the fairy tale which MacDonald embedded within *At the Back of the North Wind*. The shifts between social concerns, realism, fantasy and the employment of the genre of fairy tale are characteristic of MacDonald's work. Yuko Ashitagawa's "Differences and Similarities: 'Little Daylight' and 'The Light Princess'" problematises the critical positioning of texts within overall generic classifications, such as fairy tale. She argues that in doing so aspects particular to that specific text may be overlooked or masked by over emphasis on the notion of genre.

Larry E. Fink's essay "Natural History--the Heavenly Sort: George MacDonald's Integration of Faith and Reason" shifts the line of discussion to a closer consideration of MacDonald's philosophical positioning situating MacDonald's approaches to notions of evolution both from the perspectives of the physical and the spiritual. Through close reference to textual evidence Larry Fink points out MacDonald's questioning approach to received thinking, and his attitude of integration in matters pertaining to faith and reason, religion and science. One could take the previous phrase concerning the questioning, probing mind of the thinker and writer and as readily apply it to the influential and acclaimed contemporary author Philip Pullman. William Gray discusses notions of authorial relationship in "MacDonald and Pullman, or: (Great-great-) grandfather George" which considers discontinuity as well as commonalities. Gray includes C.S. Lewis in this chronological continuum, since Lewis strongly acknowledged the influence of MacDonald. Interestingly Lewis is an "antagonist" for Pullman, however, as William Blake observed "Without contraries is no progression" (William Blake *Marriage of Heaven and Hell*).

Literary theory has evolved considerably during the latter stages of the twentieth century as reflected in the three readings of MacDonald's work by Maria Nikolajeva, Roderick McGillis and Elmar Schenkel, who each apply contemporary literary theory in different modes to bring deeper understanding of MacDonald's work. Maria Nikolajeva in "Voice, Gender and Alterity in George MacDonald's Fairy Tales" discusses and analyses the power balance between the adult author and the implied young audience. She further considers other strategies of alterity employed by MacDonald and the impact of such synergies. Much attention has been given per se in contemporary literary studies to gender construction and inequality, however, as Nikolajeva demonstrates, gender is not the paramount consideration in MacDonald's fairy tales, since child characters are "exchangeable as far as gender is concerned"; however, what is of paramount importance is the "adult – child axis of the power tension". The "rite of passage" is generally associated with writing for children or young adults, where the subject journeys from a position of "innocence" and lack of power to one of knowledge and empowerment. "Liminality as Psychic Stage in MacDonald's *Lilith"* by Roderick McGillis, analyses such a journey in MacDonald's second adult fantasy. McGillis' discussion of the shifts between "realities" in Vane's psychic experiences forms an interesting link with earlier essays in this collection which concentrate on reality, social conditions and other worlds of fantasy and fairy tale. The relevance of MacDonald both to child and adult audiences is thus demonstrated and one may readily read across these essays and consider the application of MacDonald's thinking and variety of narrative strategies to experiences which occur at different developmental stages in the human condition.

With regard to reading across this collection Elmar Schenkel's highly innovative consideration of MacDonald's *Lilith* (1895) and Joseph Conrad's *Heart of Darkness* (1895) draws attention to the imperialist contextualisation of both works at the end of the nineteenth century. As Schenkel observes both works "are about issues closely linked to the age of late Victorianism and its private and colonial economy" which raise awareness and questions about "the social self, society and the question of greed and power over others." Schenkel's contention is "that while MacDonald addresses these questions rather from the inside of the psyche, Conrad illuminates a moral change overcoming the individual from the outside, from actual social and geographical experience." The essays of Rod McGillis and Elmar Schenkel thus make an illuminating "paired reading" each contributing different facets to a complex argument which circulated around notions of subjectivity, and therefore place MacDonald not only as a Romantic writer (as he is predominantly critically viewed), but also as a Modernist.

Whereas the previous essays have situated MacDonald's work within the contexts of the nineteenth century and contemporary literary theory and reading, the final contributions locate MacDonald within the twenty-first century in terms of creative writing and young readership. Thom Saterlee considers implications and possibilities of the inclusion of MacDonald's fairy tale "The Wise Woman" as a model for creative writing classes, thus potentially extending the influence of MacDonald. Judith Elkin's evaluation of the importance of reading and the impact of the reading of MacDonald for contemporary young readers, drawing on illuminating research by Rachel Johnson into the child's relationship with reading MacDonald. It seems highly pertinent to conclude this collection of essays with the reader, a subject central to George MacDonald's work. In *Lilith* the character of Vane undergoes psychic experiences located within the library, experiences which formulate his rite of passage, thus linking reading directly with his formative journey. MacDonald's mode of writing and thinking which resists closure, exploring notions of subjectivity, philosophy, theology, moral and social concerns, places the reader at the open centre of the 'problem solving' complex where no absolute answers exist: the situation of the moral and intellectual life itself. MacDonald takes his reader on journeys through many worlds which traverse time and place. This collection of essays demonstrates such journeyings; his critical readership, as represented by the international body of contributors, has traversed time and place, producing some suggested answers and surely stimulating other demanding and important questions arising from the work of George MacDonald, the answers to which lie in other times and other realities.

I would like to acknowledge the support of colleagues in the production of this collection, the contributors; Maya Das, PhD research student at the University of Worcester for proof reading, and Allan Maund/Rachel Webb also at Worcester for their administrative help.

CHAPTER ONE

GEORGE MACDONALD AND SOCIAL ISSUES

DAVID L. NEUHOUSER

George MacDonald's views on various social issues such as poverty, the role of women, environmental concerns, and animal rights is evident in his life and in his extensive writings. I believe that his views on these issues are still worth consideration a century later. This paper will attempt to describe his ideas on these issues. MacDonald commented on other social issues such as race, euthanasia, war and peace but these will have to wait for a later study.

As a college student, MacDonald was influenced by a young pastor, John Kennedy, who was active in social concerns. "It was through this man Kennedy that MacDonald had his first taste of social work and his first sight of the poverty and squalor of a big city" (Raeper 51). MacDonald was later influenced by F. D. Maurice who advocated Christian Socialism. "The program these Christian (not Marxist) Socialists advocated emphasized individual responsibility as well as social reform by the application of Christian principles to all social relationships" (Hein 206).

A character in *Weighed and Wanting* says, "[T]he condition of our poor in our large towns is the great question of the day" (262). MacDonald seemed to agree with this as shown by the frequency this problem occurs in his novels. (MacDonald commonly used certain characters in his novels to express his own views. All such quotations in this paper are, I believe, expressions of his personal views,) How to help the poor, though, is a difficult question for money alone is not the answer. In the *Seaboard Parish* he says, "Nothing is more difficult than to make money useful to the poor" (107). Statements like this abound in MacDonald's writing. "The first question is not how to do good with money, but how to keep from doing evil with it. Money is important as dynamite is important – mainly because it is exceedingly dangerous" (*Castle Warlock,* 364). However, "It [money] is powerful for good when divinely used" (*Paul Faber* 33). And, money should be used to help the poor. "Certainly the rich withdraw themselves from the poor. Instead, for instance, of helping them to bear their burdens, they leave the still struggling poor of whole parishes to sink into hopeless want" (*The Vicar's Daughter* 177). Also in *Paul Faber*, the answer to a wealthy man who asks what he should first do with his money to try to set things right for the poor is, "I should say *injustice*. My very soul revolts against the talk about kindness to the poor, when such a great part of their misery comes from the injustice and greed of the rich" (185-6).

One problem that MacDonald had with just giving money to the poor was that it might make them dependent on gifts and they might not know how to use it wisely. "[Y]ou ought not to give them anything they *ought* to provide for themselves, such as food or clothing or shelter." (*The Vicar's Daughter* 163). He qualifies this statement by saying that it is okay to provide food, clothing, or shelter if they are unable to do so. And he suggests that something unexpected like flowers might be given!

A personal relation with the poor is necessary before giving alms.

> When compassion itself is precious to a man . . . it must be because he loves you, and believes you love him. When that is the case, you may give him any thing you like, and it will do neither you nor him harm. But the man of independent feeling, except he be thus your friend, will not unlikely resent your compassion, while the beggar will accept it chiefly as a pledge for something more to be got from you; and so it will tend to keep him in beggary (*The Vicar's Daughter* 163).

This theme of personal relations runs through all of his books and is best exemplified by the character Robert Falconer in the book of the same name. Falconer works in the slums of London and gets to know the people before attempting to help. He does co-operate with others but rejects any kind of official organization and firmly believes that money is worse than useless except as a genuine outcome of human feelings and brotherly love. Falconer is a doctor and studies law so that he can help the poor with legal matters, that is, to help them to receive justice. *Robert Falconer* was "an exposé of London slums that helped transform social work in England" (Amell 15). As a result of reading the book, many young people in England went to London to work in the slums.

Here is a description of one of Falconer's schemes

> To provide suitable dwellings for the poor he considered the most pressing of all necessary reforms. His own fortune was not sufficient for doing much in this way, but he set about doing what he could by purchasing houses in which the poor lived, and putting them into the hands of persons whom he could trust, and who were immediately responsible to him for their proceedings: they had to make them fit for human abodes, and let them to those who desired better accommodation, giving the preference to those already tenants, so long as they paid their reasonable rent, which he considered far more necessary for them to do than for him to have done (*Falconer* 372).

This housing scheme is very similar to that of his friend, John Ruskin and Octavia Hill. Ruskin put up the money to buy up property and hired Hill to manage it. In *The Vicar's Daughter*, Clare is a character who lives in the slums of London and helps the poor with financial aid from Lady Bernard. Clare's character is based on Octavia Hill; and Lady Bernard's partly on Lady Byron who gave financial assistance to the MacDonalds and partly on John Ruskin who financed Hill. In *Robert Falconer*, he said that one of the reasons for poor housing was, "the rapacity of the holders of small house-property, and the utter wickedness of railway companies, who pulled down every house that stood in their way, and did nothing to provide room for those who were thus ejected – most probably from a wretched place, but only to be driven into a more wretched still" (372).

Octavia Hill (1838-1912) was a close personal friend of the MacDonald family and her ideas about the problems of poverty were remarkably like MacDonald's. She was the "leader of the British open-space movement, which resulted in the foundation (1895) of the National Trust for Places of Historic Interest or Natural Beauty. She was also a housing reformer whose methods of housing project management were imitated in Great Britain, on the Continent, and in the United States" (*The New Encyclopaedia Britannica*, 1998). She not only managed housing so that poor people could afford it, she ministered holistically to their physical, social, educational, and spiritual needs. "The 'Octavia Hill system" as it became known, was summed up by Lord Salisbury as; "to improve the tenants with the tenements" (Whelan 5).

Octavia had definite ideas about how to help the poor. Her parents and grandfather had experience of working for those in need and F. D. Maurice influenced her ideas. She believed that her housing projects should not be gifts to the poor, but should make a 5% profit for the investor. (This 5% figure is the same as that in the housing project in *The Vicar's Daughter*.) There were two reasons for this. She wanted her work to be copied by others who would not do so if they did not make money, but, more importantly, the poor should have the satisfaction of being able to take care of themselves. The spiritual and moral welfare of the people was more important than their physical welfare. This did not mean that the rich had no responsibility. In fact, they had more. They must help the poor to learn to manage and must help provide work that paid a living wage. In other words, the privileged should work to get rid of injustice.

In an article which Octavia wrote in 1872, she said, "If the poor are to be raised to a permanently better position they must be dealt with as individuals and by individuals" (Bell 200). She always worked personally with her tenants and got to know them and they her. Later, as her work expanded to hundreds of houses and thousands of tenants, she trained other workers to have individual relations with those she was trying to help. In his novel *Robert Falconer*,

MacDonald uses his hero to express his ideas about charitable work, ideas which were similar to Octavia's that he could work with individuals only, not with classes.

One example, which is illustrative of Hill's method of encouraging responsibility on the part of her tenants, is given in the following quotation:

> She told them all how much money she had to spend on repairs in each house, and promised that if the actual cost of necessary repairs fell short of the sum she had put aside, the balance should be spent on any improvement they desired, safes, washing stools, copper lids or cupboards, the choice should be theirs. At once it became the interest of all to keep the repairs bill low; wanton damage ceased at once, accidents became fewer, and many of the men became interested in doing repairs themselves to save money (Bell 83).

One of her principles was that she would first of all make the housing sound and hygienic and do nothing more until she was sure that the tenants would value and not abuse the added improvements.

There is an interesting example of how MacDonald used Octavia's experiences in his novels. It also shows that there is some truth in the old adage that "truth is stranger than fiction." In *Robert Falconer*, the hero offers a landlord enough money to buy his building but is refused. The owner admits that he cannot make that much money from rents. However, he is also an undertaker and says:

> "But it's the funerals, sir, that make it worth my while... I count back-rent in the burying. People may cheat their landlord, but they can't cheat the undertaker. They *must* be buried. That's the one indispensable – ain't it, sir?" (*Robert Falconer* 373)

When I first read that, I thought it was unrealistic. Then I read Octavia Hill's biography and found that it was a true story. She was told by a landlord-undertaker, "Yes Miss, of course there are plenty of bad debts. It's not the rents I look to, but the deaths I get out of the houses!" (Boyd, 107)

In *Weighed and Wanting*, a character says that many are talking about the question of how to help the poor, but "if all who found the question interesting would instead of talking about it do what they could . . . to its removal they would at least make their mark, . . . of which not all the wind of words would in ten thousand years blow away a spadeful" (262-3). The question arises, however, as to whether George MacDonald only talked about the problem or whether he did do something about it? The following demonstrates that he was a man of action as well as words.

MacDonald often went to Octavia Hill's housing projects to speak to the tenants. Due to his sincerity and ability to treat them as equals many responded positively as he read them his fairy tales and used moral anecdotes in order to teach them about Christ. The MacDonald family often had "entertainments" (food, music, drama) at their home in London for their friends. However, there were "large numbers of underprivileged people who came to the 'entertainments'." These were "mostly from among Octavia Hill's tenants" (Hein 206). In fact, MacDonald's wealthy friends would serve the underprivileged at these "entertainments." After one of these occasions, MacDonald apologized to John Ruskin for keeping him so busy serving the poor that Ruskin's needs were not met.

Penniless persons or drunkards were taken in by the MacDonald family and helped, sometimes successfully and sometimes not. A young mother of two girls, divorced and disowned by her husband, was cared for by the MacDonalds until her death and then they raised her daughters. They also took in other orphans for indefinite periods of time and treated them as part of the family. He would also "occasionally waive a speaking fee for lectures . . . donating his services for a worthy cause. . . [For example,] at an 1887 lecture in Bristol on *King Lear*, the proceeds from ticket sales were donated to a 'ragged school' for the poor" (Amell 27).

A second issue to be considered is the rôle of women. MacDonald's view of women is also shown in his novels and fairy tales. In the fairy tales the God figure is always a woman; the foremost examples of which are the Wise Woman in *The Wise Woman* and the great grandmother, Irene, in both of the Curdie stories. In his novel *Castle Warlock*, he has Cosmo's father say that God is "father and mother both to all men" (18). Interestingly in his realistic novels, a man is often the "ideal Christian." However, there are exceptions, the most notable being Janet Grant in *Sir Gibbi* where she is described as prophetess (9) and priestess (170) not only for the young Gibbie, but also for her husband. In *Weighed and Wanting*, even though Mr. Raymount was a university graduate and a successful author, his wife is described as "half the head and more than half the heart of [the] family" (9).

MacDonald was aware of the low status of women in Victorian England as shown by the following remark by a character in *Phantastes,* "I dare say you know something of your great-grandfathers a good deal . . . but you know very little about your great-grandmothers on either side" (18). In many of his novels he has women studying subjects that were not considered appropriate for women at that time. For example in *Castle Warlock*, Aggie understood algebra and geometry better than the hero of the novel and she was physically stronger as well as shown by a snowstorm incident:

> Aggie was more than a match for Cosmo: smaller and stronger in proportion to her size, she bored her way through the blast better than he. The moment he

began to expostulate she would increase the distance between them until she could not hear a sound he uttered. (*Castle Warlock* 73).

Beyond his writing MacDonald again "put words into action", for he taught mathematics and science in women's colleges. He also taught his future sister-in-law mathematics. She was considered, in her own words, "the fool of the family," but she said that MacDonald "understood me as an equal" (Greville 98).

MacDonald believed that there are feminine and masculine characteristics. In *Malcolm* he wrote, "By no words can I express my scorn of the evil fancy that the distinction between them [the sexes] is solely or even primarily physical" (80). For example, he thought women were keener of perception than men (*Castle Warlock* 51). George would have been proud of his son Greville who wrote, "If I say my mother had beyond most women masculine courage, it is to name her the nobler woman: if I find my father gifted beyond most men with feminine pity, it proclaims him the greater man" (Greville 338). (George's wife, Louisa, was, without doubt, one of the reasons he had such a high opinion of women. She was a strong woman who raised eleven children, nursed George through many illnesses, and even wrote and directed plays put on by the family to raise needed finances.) George MacDonald praises one of his fictional characters for his "mingling of manly confidence with feminine trustfulness" (*St. George and St. Michael*, 109). In other words, MacDonald believed that some characteristics were feminine and some masculine but both men and women were better men and better women if each had both kinds of characteristics. An interesting comment about how these masculine and feminine characteristics combined in male and female is found in *David Elginbrod* where he referred to, "The beauty of [David] . . . and the wondrous loveliness which he had transmitted from the feminine part of his nature to the wholly feminine and therefore delicately powerful nature of [his daughter]" (*David Elginbrod* 319).

According to his biographer William Raeper, "in many ways he [MacDonald] was . . . liberal even feminist" (Raeper 259). However, there were limitations which crept into MacDonald's thinking on the subject of women, for in *The Seaboard Parish*, he wrote:

> And here I may remark in regard to one of the vexed questions of the day – the rights of women–that what women demand it is not for men to withhold. It is not their business to lay down the law for women. That women must lay down for themselves. I confess that, although I must herein seem to many of my readers old-fashioned and conservative, I should not like to see any woman I cared much for either in parliament or in an anatomical class-room; but on the other hand I feel that women must be left free to settle that matter. If it is not

good, good women will find it out and recoil from it. If it is good, then God give them good speed. One thing they *have* a right to – a far wider and more valuable education than they have been in the way of receiving. (*The Seaboard Parish* 291).

He wrote this passage in 1868. By 1871 he had changed his mind about the medical education of women, perhaps as a result of meeting Elizabeth Garrett Anderson, the first woman doctor. At that time "he signed a letter along with Florence Nightingale, James Balfour and Charles Darwin" and others in favour of a petition for rendering possible the medical education of women (Raeper 260).

His friend Octavia Hill did not favour women's suffrage partly because she thought that political equality with men might lower the number of volunteers for charitable work and probably because she believed that it was not the solution to the problem of gender inequality. In *Mary Marston*, MacDonald wrote, "But the thing will be set right one day, and in a better fashion than if all the women's rights' committees in the world had their will of the matter" (208). I suspect that both MacDonald and Hill believed that laws would cause more antagonism between the sexes and that individual minds and hearts had to be changed. In his personal life, however, MacDonald may not have been entirely consistent about gender equality. For example, biographies of MacDonald indicate that he seemed more concerned about his sons' education than that of his daughters'. This may have been a necessary concession to the society and economic structure of his day.

I now wish to consider concerns about the environment and the use or misuse of technology. MacDonald was concerned about protecting the environment. He loved nature and in one of his literary essays he wrote about the importance of keeping open eyes "for the sweet fashionings and blendings of her [nature's] operation around him" (*A Dish of Orts* 41). Furthermore he believed that greed was a cause for the "hideous lacerations and vile gatherings of refuse which . . . disfigure the earth" (*Malcolm* 344). He had some very strong words about the men who caused these environmental problems.

> May the ghosts of the men who mar the earth, turning her sweet rivers into channels of filth, and her living air into irrespirable vapours and pestilences, haunt the desolations they have made, until they loathe the work of their hands and turn from themselves with a divine repudiation. (*Malcolm* 344).

MacDonald appreciated and enjoyed technology but understood its drawbacks as well as its benefits. There is a wonderful character in *St. George and St. Michael*, Lord Herbert, who is a creative inventor. One of his inventions was a "water commanding engine" about which the inventor claimed, "herewith may marshland be thoroughly drained, or dry land perfectly watered; great cities kept sweet and wholesome," and be "beneficial to all mankind" (*St. George and St. Michael* 133-4). However, the narrator in the novel comments:

> Little did Lord Herbert dream of the age he was initiating – of the irreverence and pride and destruction that was about to follow in his footsteps, wasting, defiling, searing, obliterating, turning beauty into ashes and worse! That divine mechanics should thus, through selfishness and avarice be leagued with squalor and ugliness: . . . What would the inventor of the water-commanding engine have said to the pollution of our waters, the destruction of the very landmarks of our history, the desecration of ruins that ought to be venerated for their loveliness as well as their story! (430-1)

MacDonald's concerns also extended to animal rights. "[He] devoted entire written sermons to denouncing cruelty to animals" (Amell 103). In many of his novels characters are condemned for their mistreatment of animals. He loved animals, especially horses and even believed that they would be in heaven. He lost his first and only pastorate partly because of a sermon on the possibility that some animals might have eternal life. This position was also advocated by his most famous twentieth century disciple, C. S. Lewis.

Vivisection was another of MacDonald's concerns. "Part of [the] novel, *Paul Faber, Surgeon* was reprinted as an anti-vivisection tract" (Raeper 175). MacDonald must have discussed this issue with his good friend Lewis Carroll who wrote an essay, "Some Popular Fallacies about Vivisection," (reprinted in *The Complete Works of Lewis Carroll)* which was a logical analysis of the problem. An essay by C. S. Lewis entitled "Vivisection," appears in *God in the Dock* and has views quite similar to MacDonald's.

To conclude, in all of the positions that MacDonald took on these issues, he was obviously influenced by the opinions and prejudices of his time but I believe that on most issues he held a more enlightened view than most of his contemporaries. His ideas show worthwhile insights that are still valuable in any thoughtful consideration of the problems today.

Works Cited

All of the following books by George MacDonald are available as reprints from Johannesen, P.O. Box 24, Whitethorn, CA 95589.
All of the quotations from George MacDonald's books are from the editions published by Johannesen.

MacDonald. George. *Castle Warlock*, Kegan Paul, Trench, Trubner & Co. 4th edition, London, 1890

—. *David Elginbrod*, Mackay, Philadelphia, 1900.
—. *Dish of Orts*, Sampson Low, Marston & Co., London, 1895.
—. *Malcolm*, Kegan Paul, London, 1886.
—. *The Marquis of Lossie*, Kegan Paul, London, 1887
—. *Mary Marston*, Sampson Low, Marston, Searle, & Rivington, London, 1881.
—. *Paul Faber, Surgeon*, George Routledge & Sons, New York, 1900
—. *Phantastes*, Arthur C. Fields, London, 1905.
—. Robert Falconer, Hurst & Blackett, 1880.
—. The Seaboard Parish, Strahan, London, 1869.
—. *Sir Gibbie*, A. L. Burt, NY, 1900.
—. *St. George and St. Michael*, C. Kegan Paul & Co., London, 1878.
—. *The Vicar's Daughter*, Little, Brown, & Co., Boston, 1899.
—. *Weighed and Wanting*, Sampson Low, Marston, Searle & Rivington, London, 1882.
Amell, Barbara. *The Art of God*: Portland, OR: Wingfold Books, 2004.
Bell, E. Moberly. Octavia Hill, London: Constable & Co. Ltd., 1943.
Boyd, Nancy. *Three Victorian Women Who Changed Their World,* NY/Oxford: Oxford University Press, 1982.
Hein, Rolland, *George MacDonald: Victorian Mythmaker*, Nashville, Tennessee: Star Song Publishing Group, 1993,
Maurice, C. Edmund. *Life of Octavia Hill as told in her letters*, London: Macmillan and Co. Limited, 1914.
Raeper, William, *George MacDonald*, Tring, Herts, England: Lion Publishing plc. 1987.
Whelan, Robert, ed. *Octavia Hill and the Social Housing Debate: Essays and Letters by Octavia Hill*, Public Institute of Economic Affairs: Health and Welfare Unit. Bury St. Edmonds, Suffolk, U. K. 1998.

CHAPTER TWO

REALISM, FANTASY AND A CRITIQUE
OF NINETEENTH CENTURY SOCIETY
IN GEORGE MACDONALD'S
AT THE BACK OF THE NORTH WIND

JEAN WEBB

George MacDonald's *At the Back of the North Wind,* (1871) can be situated between two seemingly opposite lines of literary evolution in English literature in the nineteenth century: the realist social problem novel, as exemplified by Elizabeth Gaskell's novel for adults, *Mary Barton*, (1848) and the burgeoning of fantasy writing for children in the 1870s, for example Charles Kingsley's *The Water Babies* (1863), and Lewis Carroll's *Alice in Wonderland* (1864). Kingsley and Carroll have been designated under the title of writers of "Nonsense", however, embedded in their work is a critique of 19th century society. Similarly MacDonald is perceived as a writer of fantasy, and similarly MacDonald engages in a philosophical and moral discussion and critique of the contemporary Victorian English society.

In her novel *Mary Barton* Elizabeth Gaskell was intent upon raising awareness of the deplorable conditions under which the poor lived in Manchester in the 1840s. Such conditions were also recorded by Friedrich Engels in his journeys around England at the time[i]. In terms of design of the city, (as in London), Manchester was particular in that due to the ergonomic patterns it need not be necessary for the rich to come into contact with the poor, since they lived and worked in separate areas. Gaskell was married to a Unitarian Minister, thus her work would have taken her into the places shunned by others of the middle classes. She also demonstrated a high level of moral and social conscience and a sensibility towards the ignored poor. Benjamin Disraeli had previously brought such division to the notice of the reading public in his novel *Sybil or The Two Nations* (1845) stating that England was comprised of two nations, the rich and the poor.

In her Preface to *Mary Barton* Elizabeth Gaskell ponders on the lives of the poor as follows:

> I had always felt a deep sympathy with the care-worn men, who looked as if doomed to struggle through their lives in strange alternations between work and want, tossed to and fro by circumstance, apparently in a greater degree than other men.
> (*Mary Barton* xxxv)

> [...] I bethought me how deep might be the innocence of some of those who elbowed me daily in the streets of the town in which I resided.
> (*Mary Barton* xxxvi)

Gaskell demonstrates an humanitarian approach to the poor, setting the lives of her characters in the turbulent social and political contexts of the 1840s which was a decade of boom and bust in manufacturing. The Chartist Movement was also pushing for the franchise for working class men. Gaskell's characters are fully engaged in the political action, the tension and understandable dissatisfaction which led to riot and social unrest. Again she records this awareness in her Preface:

> I saw they were sore and more irritable against the rich, the even tenor of whose seemingly happy lives appeared to increase the anguish caused by the lottery-like nature of their own.
> (*Mary Barton* xxxv)

Thus her protagonists struggle with the poverty of their everyday working lives and strive for the movement towards greater political equality. Disraeli also focussed on political economy and the impact such had on the working classes. Both writers had strong moral and humanitarian drives underpinning their work, which they integrated into the realist depiction of their characters and the decisions they made.

By the 1870s some movement had been made in the improvement of working conditions and the franchise, however, there was still much to be done, especially in social conditions for the poor. Charles Kingsley's *The Water Babies,* (1863), brought the plight of the child chimney sweeps to the notice of the reading public. Kingsley's novel is a combination of realism, fairytale and the surreal, as the narrator observes Tom on his journey of moral redemption from boy chimney sweep, to water baby, to a Great Man of Science. *The Water Babies* is also a critique of nineteenth century society, in terms of the cruelties and working conditions for these child sweeps (for some of them were girls), and of the morality of the contemporary world. A great work in the genre of fantasy and surrealism, Kingsley's intention is not to explore the nature of the

Realism, Fantasy and a Critique of Nineteenth Century Society in George MacDonald's *At the Back of the North Wind*

imagination as was that of George MacDonald, who, amongst other matters, was concerned with morality, both social and individual, and the nature of humanity. Kingsley's fantasy world was a parallel one, for characters and related events from the "real" world are transposed and continued into the fantasy creation which translates the debates of the period, and those Kingsley was having with himself concerning Darwinism, for example, and notions of creation. Kingsley does not offer any practical solutions. His answers lie in the morality of the individual; the moral education of Tom. In *At the Back of the North Wind*, the agent for change is Diamond, who is morally pure and innocent. MacDonald's world of fantasy is better described as an adjunct world, for Diamond moves to the back of the North Wind, yet the happenings there are not observed by the reader, nor can Diamond clearly transpose such into reality. This country lies within the imagination of the reader, and is recalled by Diamond through the poetry and music he brings back with him as a memory of his experiences.

George MacDonald's essay 'The Fantastic Imagination' (1893) can be read in conjunction with *At the Back of the North Wind*, as a discussion of the imagination which enlightens the reading of MacDonald's novel for children. In 'The Fantastic Imagination' he writes:

> The natural world has its laws, and no man must interfere with them in the way of presentment any more than in the way of use
>
> a man may, if he pleases, invent a little world of his own, with its own laws ('Fantastic Imagination' 5)

which is what he does in the novel, both in his realist creation and in the world beyond the North Wind. MacDonald's discursive thoughts relate to the narrative structure of *At the Back of the North Wind*. There are no magical happenings which change the real world for the better; all change is derived from a logical cause and effect mode conducive to realist writing. The inclusion of the North Wind enables MacDonald to invent "a little world of his own" for the interaction of Diamond and the North Wind in order to explore the otherness of the imagination; yet even that world does not transgress the laws which govern over both reality and imagination, as will be discussed further. What is enhanced by Diamond's interaction with the North Wind is his ability to effect change by the ambiance of his personality. Despite the desperations of poverty into which Diamond and his family descend, Diamond creates harmony. Here there is a direct relationship with MacDonald's theorising on the writing of fantasy:

His world once invented, the highest law that comes next into play is, that there shall be harmony between the laws by which the new world has begun to exist;
('Fantastic Imagination' 6)

The root of such harmony is with Diamond's close relationship with the natural world, epitomised in the personification of the North Wind.

In his introductory paragraph MacDonald emphasises the difference between his conceptualisation of the back of the North Wind and that recorded by Herodotus, which suggests that it was "so comfortable" that "a people who lived there" "drowned themselves" (*North Wind* 11). A playful implication here is that Herodotus, who is regarded as a founding father of historians, actually got it wrong. This is especially ironic in that the Victorian period was one particularly interested in the formulation of the writing of history, with the work of Thomas Carlyle et al. A further implication is that an excess of "comfort" cannot be transposed into the real world, which is certainly not the case in MacDonald's text, for Diamond brings great comfort to all who know him.

Diamond's sleeping accommodation in a room over the coach-house where Old Diamond, the horse is stabled is not comfortable by modern standards but it is so for the boy because he is in close proximity to nature. He luxuriates in the warmth and smell of the hay and the security of the horse below. MacDonald's description of the flimsiness of the boards which separate his sleeping quarters from the outside world and the domain of the North Wind is emphasised by the image of the wind slipping through the slit in the boards made by a penknife like a "cat after a mouse" (*North Wind* 11). The closeness to nature is thereby introduced and gently stressed from the very beginnings of the narrative. Furthermore, and more importantly, Diamond is closer to the horse rather than to his family in those private hours, when he settles and sleeps, and it is with the horse that he shares a close understanding and relationship. Even their name is shared. Horse and boy; boy and horse become synonymous, as it were. Yet interestingly, MacDonald elected to limit this relationship to one which refused to enter into say, magical conversations between the two. The equine Diamond is an instrumental factor in the realist narrative, not the fantasy. The greater force of Nature embodied in the North Wind which surrounds both boy and horse is the conduit into the world of the imagination.

Diamond's first experience of meeting North Wind is one which develops through natural association. She emerges as a presence firstly in her "normally" natural state:

> The wind was rising again, and getting very loud, and full of rushes and whistles. (*North Wind* 13)

The logical development is the emergence of a voice, that of North Wind herself. Structurally the narrative is rational, easing the reader from realism into fantasy and the imagination. MacDonald abides by the classical unities of time, place and character, in strong contrast to the fantasy creations of his contemporary, Lewis Carroll whose *Alice in Wonderland* certainly has it's own logical construction which is based on syllogism and moving beyond the constraints of time and place[ii]. MacDonald's technique dissolves those boundaries, fusing together the real and fantasy worlds, thus conveying that sense of the imaginary/fantasy space which can be in the actual as well as another place.

> From his first sight of North Wind, Diamond is "entranced with her mighty beauty" (*North Wind* 18).

The physical description MacDonald assigns to North Wind brilliantly produces a solidity out of the wind which as Christina Rossetti observed in her poem "Who has seen the wind?" (1893) could only normally be materialised in the effect on objects, such as the trees. MacDonald's personification of the wind is a combination of physical attributes, such as her flowing hair and the description of her face which looked "out of the midst of it like a moon out of a cloud" (*North Wind* 18).

Their conversation had circulated upon Diamond's unusual name, which North Wind thought "funny" (*North Wind* 16), a response to which Diamond objects. The expectation of the reader in association with the word 'diamond' is to think of the precious stone, however, for Diamond his connection is with the 'great and good horse' (*North Wind* 17). Both of them have to come to know each other, further than the representation of their names; as MacDonald comments: "For to know a person's name is not always to know the person's self" (*North Wind* 17), – which in many ways is the crux of the text, for MacDonald is creating a child protagonist who will mean more than the materialistic associations with his name. In fact the character of Diamond is a rejection of the materialism and capitalism which drove and blighted human experience in the Victorian period, and which in many ways still does today.

North Wind logically has to be a beautiful woman, for as MacDonald wrote in 'The Fantastic Imagination':

> Law is the soil in which alone beauty will grow; beauty is the only stuff in which Truth can be clothed; and you may, if you will, call Imagination the tailor that cuts her garments to fit her'
> ('Fantastic Imagination' 6).

Beauty, Law and the Imagination are fused together in the figure of North Wind. Through their interaction Diamond is initiated and educated into such understanding, which he will disseminate to those with whom he communicates. Following his first meeting with North Wind, Diamond is found in the courtyard and taken into the warmth of the drawing-room, for they think he has been sleep-walking. He mistakenly thinks that Miss Coleman is his North Wind, and is then disappointed. Here the fusion between reality and imagination is emphasized; the transposition of the world of fantasy back into reality, which is then in itself unsatisfactory. The process of moving into the fantasy world is gradual and logical: a child's dream, perhaps, on a stormy night, or the initiation into an other worldliness which exists outside normality.

Diamond's next meeting with North Wind is pre-figured by his return to the yard where North Wind had left him. Having been confined to home because of bad weather for a week, his experience of going outside to play before sunset is one of a bountiful re-union with nature. He is described as "flying from the door like a bird from its cage" (*North Wind* 31). MacDonald provides a luscious description of the sunset over the stable-yard:

> And Diamond thought that, next to his own home, he had never seen any place he would like so much to live in as that sky.
> (*North Wind* 31).

MacDonald is bringing together the elements of the narrative in a logical construction, so that it is acceptable when Diamond is so happy at the back of the North Wind, and that he is deeply embedded in the love of his family. What is also emphasized is the Romantic relationship with nature. Diamond is a Romantic child; he is emotionally affected by his natural surroundings; an innocent who moves from innocence to experience through both his relationships with North Wind, in terms of the imagination, the spiritual, and with those he meets and affects in his "real" life.

The world of the imagination is brought into Diamond's consciousness and confirmed as being part of his reality when he returns to the yard and remembers "how the wind had driven him to the same spot on the night of his dream" (*North Wind* 31). He stoops down to look at a primrose, "a dwarfish thing", focussing on the diminutive size of the plant, which is itself stirred by a "little wind" (North Wind31). The centre of the primrose is described as being "one eye that the dull black wintry earth had opened to look at the sky with" (*North Wind* 31). In his own way, Diamond will be an eye through which his family and close companions will be "able to look at the sky" or rather "into" the sky when he recounts later his journey to the back of the North Wind. Diamond will become the "eye" through which others may see.

Realism, Fantasy and a Critique of Nineteenth Century Society in George MacDonald's *At the Back of the North Wind*

The emphasis on size in this passage is an instrumental introduction to the changing size and power of the North Wind. She is diminutive at sunset, in this case, and will grow to a mighty raging storm, as we all change in emotional power at different points of experience. The primrose acts as a referent in the later conversation which Diamond has with North Wind:

> "But you're no bigger than me."
> "Do you think I care how big or how little I am? Didn't you see me this evening. I was less then."
> "No. Where was you?"
> "Behind the leaves of the primrose. Didn't you see them blowing?"
> "Yes."
> (*North Wind* 33).

North Wind's ability to change size is a responsive approach to the demands of natural conditions, rather than the happenstance of changes in body size to which Carroll's Alice is subjected. Diamond is also, through such conversations and experiences with North Wind, learning of the multiplicity of the self. As an aside, I also think that the analogy with the North Wind and the variations in levels of energy in response to situations, parallels the levels of energy, both emotional and intellectual which one may feel "inside one's head" at different times, and the energies created by engagement with the creative imagination. Physically, emotionally and spiritually we are not static beings.

North Wind is certainly not static, as said. Diamond accompanies her on a journey through the environs, as her energy increases she becomes a "full-grown girl" (*North Wind* 35) and then a wolf which frightens a drunken woman who should have been caring for a child. Here MacDonald incorporates a direct moral warning against the excesses of drink, whilst also including a discussion of the perception of "good" and "bad" and the differences between person and necessary action. Following her appearance as a wolf North Wind comments to Diamond:

> "Good people see good things; bad people, bad things."
> "Then are you a bad thing?"
> "No. For *you* see me, Diamond, dear," said the girl, and she looked down at him, and Diamond saw the loving eyes of the great lady beaming from the depths of her falling hair.
> (*North Wind* 36).

Diamond's relationship with the North Wind is an educative one. In the episodes in the "real" world Diamond is given broadening experiences which he may not fully understand, because they lie outside of the rationality in which

Diamond can operate, and also how as human beings we cannot 'know' the reasons for everything. Time spent with North Wind is not always comfortable and easy; he has to learn to trust her, to develop a Keatsian negative capability in not being able to "know" the rational answers to natural disasters, such as the sinking of the passenger ship. The emotional veracity of MacDonald's writing communicates how Diamond has to struggle with his doubts and fears, until he can fully trust North Wind. Initially lessons to develop this confidence in her are placed in the real world, later this trust will transpose directly to the imagined world at the back of the North Wind, where there will be no direct contact with recognised reality. MacDonald thereby takes his reader on a process of learning as he does with Diamond, and in so doing to learn more about urban society and morality, or in many cases the lack of it. Trust is established through the physical relationship between Diamond and the North Wind. On, for example, the stormy night in London, she weaves her hair together to make a warm nest for him.

> It was just like a pocket, or like the shawl in which gypsy women carry their children. (*North Wind* 38).

North Wind is a "natural" nomad, a gypsy of the sky. Diamond is technically flying with her, in the quasi-situation of being her baby cradled on her back, safe from the elemental furore below, which she is creating.

> There was a great roaring, for the wind was dashing against London like a sea; but at North Wind's back, Diamond, of course felt nothing of it at all. (*North Wind* 39).

On being questioned as to the cause of the noise, North Wind replies gently:

> "The noise of my besom. I am the old woman that sweeps the cobwebs from the sky; only I'm busy with the floor now."
> (*North Wind* 39).

The logical link is established between this moment with North Wind and seeing the little sweeper girl, struggling against the wind, dragging her broom, for it is Nanny who will figure so greatly later in the realist part of the narrative. Diamond asks if North Wind will help the child, however, at that time there are other duties for his guardian companion, who answers saying that she must not leave her work. His question is one born of his compassionate nature: "But why shouldn't you be kind to her?" North Wind points out that she is actually helping the child in one way by "sweeping the wicked smells away" (*North Wind* 41).

It will later be the influence of Diamond's kindness which saves Nanny's life and brings her a better way of living. The implied lesson communicated by North Wind is that there are actions which are appropriate at certain times, and others which are not. Here North Wind is employing a broad brush, to cleanse the city; Diamond will later employ his compassionate nature to, as it were, cleanse little Nanny's life of the tawdry lifestyle with her grandmother. MacDonald is also, through such narrative sequencing, demonstrating the cause and effect between events which may seem minor, or meetings which may be fleeting, or coincidental and then develop into important and life changing relationships.

In order to fully be prepared for the ways in which Diamond's life will change, for example, when he takes over his father's cab driving business, Diamond has to learn physical courage. The early episode in the cathedral is where North Wind tests Diamond; on trusting her; trusting his own senses and trusting his own measure of courage. North Wind leads him into one of the towers and onto a gallery to wait for her while she has to go about her duty of sinking the ship, He is, understandably, greatly afraid of falling. North Wind questions his seemingly irrational fear, for he had not quavered when nestled in her hair traversing the skies but a few moments previously. Although he is now being held by her he is upset because he is walking on his own legs, which might slip. Even though he directly states that he does not like this albeit knowing that she would be down after him and save him should he slip, North Wind lets go of his hand, wherewith Diamond screams and is "bent double with terror". "She left the words, 'Come after me', sounding in his ears." (*North Wind* 68).

The Biblical echoes here are very strong of Christ calling his disciples to demonstrate their faith in Him, to leave their normal lives and follow. The phrasing of this short sentence is also interesting, for the situation of the command is within Diamond as a physical presence. MacDonald could have more conventionally written: "North Wind called Diamond to follow her", however, this phrase would not have carried the emotive weight of the fear Diamond is entrapped by and which is within him. At such heightened traumatic moments, one does experience differently; time slows, sound becomes transposed into one's physicality, that fusion of event and emotion and the body. Diamond does survive and "pass" this test, for he walks alone, whilst realising that he had been helped by the wind blowing into his face to make him brave. She did not hold him, but she had not left him. As North Wind says afterwards:

> "You had to be taught what courage was. And you couldn't know what it was without feeling it: therefore it was given you. But don't you feel as if you would try to be brave yourself next time?"
> "Yes, I do. But trying is not much."

"Yes, it is – a very great deal, for it is a beginning. And a beginning is the greatest thing of all."
(*North Wind* 70).

North Wind passes on great wisdom to the young Diamond. The narrative structure of MacDonald's novel also imparts the philosophical perceptions which he discusses in "The Fantastic Imagination". Diamond has overcome a great fear of falling; he has discovered courage within himself, a courage which was dormant, for as MacDonald states in his essay:

> The best thing you can do for your fellow, next to raising his consciousness, is – not to give him things to think about, but to wake things up that are in him; or say, to make him think things for himself.
> ('Fantastic Imagination' 9)

The conversation between North Wind and Diamond which follows the incident on the ledge demonstrates that there cannot be absolute understanding of all states, events and consequences. They discuss how the breath of North Wind had the power to awaken courage in Diamond:

> I knew it would make you strong.....But how my breath has that power I cannot tell. It was put into me when I was made. That is all I know.'
> (*North Wind* 70).

Interestingly North Wind "knows" the power, but cannot "tell"; she is unable to articulate an explanation. Here MacDonald returns both to the rationality of his writings on the creation of the imaginary, that certain laws cannot be traversed, there has to be a logic within the created world and also to a demonstration by North Wind of negative capability. To 'know' is all she and thus Diamond, need "to know". As MacDonald states:

> In physical things a man may invent; in moral things he must obey – and take the laws with him into his invented world as well.
> ('Fantastic Imagination' 7)

Morally North Wind would have misinformed or misled Diamond had she made up a reason for why her breath has so much power. By honestly sharing her "ignorance" North Wind refrains from falsely setting herself up as all-powerful and all-knowing.

By this stage in the novel MacDonald has established a completely trusting relationship between the boy and the wind. The realist context of the harshness and inequality of nineteenth century working class life in London has also been introduced, at this point with some distance from Diamond himself, for it is later in the narrative when Diamond takes over his father's position as cab driver. The reader thus far, has an insight into Diamond's strengths and frailties, and is, in other words, getting to 'know' Diamond. High incidence of child illness and mortality was a sad reality during the nineteenth century. MacDonald's own experience and that of his family is testament to the ravages of tuberculosis, for example. Diamond's first visit to the back of the North Wind is associated with his being very ill, of the fragility of child health during the period.

MacDonald's rendering of these sections of the novel take reality–serious illness and near-death experiences, and death itself–and explore that which we cannot know through the imaginative process. Diamond is taken by his mother to Sandwich on the coast to recuperate, and to try to prevent his illness becoming more acute. He meets North Wind again in a toyshop, where she stirs the sails of a windmill. That afternoon Diamond falls very ill. He sleeps and in his doing so "found himself in a cloud of North Wind's hair" (*North Wind* 82). Body, elements and sky-scape are merged. Diamond wants to go to the back of the north wind. North Wind explains that it is not possible for her to go there, since she always blows in a southerly direction, from the north, and so she "never gets farther than the outer door" (*North Wind* 83). This is very logical, whilst being conceptually puzzling and disturbing, her namesake "home" is one she can never enter; a place of "otherness" for the North Wind herself. The way she can reach the boundary is explained by her as follows:

> "….I have only to consent to be nobody, and there I am. I draw into myself, and there I am on the doorstep."
> (*North Wind* 83).

She has to agree–with whom the reader does not know, nor needs to know– to give up her body, to become "no-body", and to relinquish her identity. The image of withdrawal is very powerful. When serious illness overtakes the individual, there is such a withdrawal from the energy of life, as portrayed by the activities of North Wind, and following the increasing withdrawal into the self, which then ceases to exist as a projection into the social world, as the patient lies in a state of suspended animation. They are a sick body with a silenced "self". Diamond travels north by sea with the aid and company of North Wind. On reaching their destination North Wind is disappearing:

> Diamond stared at her in terror, for he saw that her form and face were growing, not small, but transparent, like something dissolving not in water, but in light. He could see the side of the blue cave through her very heart.
> (*North Wind* 88).

North Wind is landscape, ice, light and nothingness, her being is all around and within her, yet she is not. Looking into the heart of light, one has all light, yet 'sees' nothing. Interestingly, for me, this pre-figures T.S. Eliot's lines in *The Wasteland*:

> ...I could not
> Speak, and my eyes failed, I was neither
> Living nor dead, and I new nothing,
> Looking into the heart of light, the silence.
> *Oed' und leer das Meer.*
> (trans. Desolate and empty the sea[iii])
> (*The Wasteland* 11 40-43).

Eliot's post-World War I image is negative and without hope, in contrast to the experiences Diamond brings back with him. At this stage, however, before he has entered that country at the back of the north wind, he has to surmount his terror, and feels that North Wind does not care for him any more.

> "Yes, I do. Only I can't show it. All my love is down at the bottom of my heart. But I feel it bubbling there."
> (*North Wind* 90).

This sums up the dilemma of the human condition, when feelings are suppressed for various reasons and the expression of love becomes concealed, lying dormant and inanimate.

MacDonald has an honesty which is communicated through the narrative voice. He addresses the reader directly, as seemingly the omniscient, all-knowing narrator, yet what he has to say is that he does not know.

> I have now come to the most difficult part of my story. And why? Because I do not know enough about it.
> (*North Wind* 91).

The narrative role is given over to Diamond who has been to the back of the north wind, whereas the "official" narrator has not. Diamond, at this point, becomes an unreliable narrator,

> Because, when he came back, he had forgotten a great deal, and what he did remember was very hard to tell. Things there are so very different from things here!
> (*North Wind 91*).

Diamond's problem is that things are so different that he has no reliable referents.

> The people there do not speak the same language for one thing. Indeed, Diamond insisted that there they do not speak at all. I do not think he was right, but it may have appeared so to Diamond.
> (*North Wind* 91).

The conversational, confiding tone of 'the' narrator is somewhat amusing, whilst also introducing a clash of power and status, between the adult narrator and the child narrator. The knowledge of Diamond is actually being overruled by someone who cannot know the truth. "The" narrator returns to the techniques derived of History and of Law: accounts given by different people which verify "the" Truth, yet in truth, verify difference according to experience. Yet again, return to the 'Fantastic Imagination' raises the philosophical and, indeed, political position of the differences in reading according to the individual reader: the liberation from a singular mode of reading and understanding.

> Everyone, however, who feels the story, will read its meaning after his own nature and development: one man will read one meaning in it, another will read another.
> ('Fantastic Imagination' 7)

Diamond's account of his experience has to be recounted by using referents with which *he* is familiar. His guide, North Wind, cannot be there with him. This has to be his interpretation and translation. The referents pertaining to the elements and landscape which MacDonald has used throughout which have enabled the description of North Wind do not exist in the same form for Diamond to use:

> The sun too had vanished; but that was no matter, for there was plenty of a certain still rayless light. Where it came from he never found out; but he thought it belonged to the country itself....He insisted that if it (the river) did not sing tunes in people's ears, it sung tunes in their heads, and proof of which I may mention that, in the troubles which followed, Diamond was often heard singing..., "One of the tunes the river at the back of the north wind sung."
> (*North Wind* 93).

The omniscient narrator is reclaiming his author-ity from Diamond by asserting that he has proof of the un-provable. MacDonald refuses to take an "easy option" with this section of recounting Diamond's memories, he could have defined the landscape at the back of the north wind, by using oppositions in a parallel world, much as Carroll did in his reversed world in *Alice Through the Looking Glass*. Instead he aligns this world beyond with this one, yet shifts the 'concreteness', giving softness to the landscape, where the river flows through grass, not rocks. There is also an emphasis on interiority as the river sings tunes "in" the head, fusing body and landscape as he has done so before.

> When Diamond is back with his mother following his visit to the back of the north wind which was in the real world of physicality a severe illness, she reads poetry to him. Despite her efforts to find a better one than the "nonsense" she has before her, "the wind blew the leaves rustling back to the same verses" (*North Wind* 110).

MacDonald is again fusing landscape, language, reality and imagination. The leaves of the book become as leaves from a tree, wind-blown and rustling.
> Now I do not know what the mother read, but this is what Diamond heard, or thought afterwards that he had heard.
> (*North Wind* 110).

The long poem is a harmonious fusion, where one element of nature flows into another linked by the repetition of words and rhythmic sounds. In his essay MacDonald discusses the relationship between music and words. His imagined opponent retorts:

> "But words are not music; words at least are meant and fitted to carry a precise meaning!"

To which MacDonald answers:

> It is very seldom indeed that they carry the exact meaning of any user of them!... Words are live things that may be variously employed to various ends.... They are things to be put together like the pieces of a dissected map, or to arrange like the notes on a stave.
> ('Fantastic Imagination' 8)

The elements of the landscape which occur in the poem – the river, shallows, hollows, dust, and daisies for example – are like the pieces of a map which becomes populated by the nesting activities of the swallows and the gambolling lambs. The river runs throughout "singing" this natural celebration of life and provides the musicality like a recurrent theme in a composition. Linguistically the poem returns to an almost repeated patterns of words like the subtle change in harmony in music. For example:

> for he loves her best
> with the nicest cakes
> which the sunshine bakes

(*North Wind* 111).

becomes a little later:

> for the nests they make
> with the clay they cake
> in the sunshine bake
> (*North Wind* 113).

The emphasis in the poem is on the musicality and harmony, rather than rationality. The patterning is repetitive and circular, the poem finishing with the lines

> and its all in the wind
> that blows from behind
> (*North Wind* 115).

MacDonald is using language in the place of music, for as he states in 'The Fantastic Imagination, using a common Romantic association between the Aeolian harp, the wind and the imagination:

> where his (the writer's) object is to move by suggestion, to cause to imagine, then let him assail the soul of the reader as the wind assails the Aeolian harp ("Fantastic Imagination"'10)

Approximately one third of the novel has been given to Diamond to reach this point, where he can realise the country at the back of the north wind in an extended poem which narrates the harmonies of nature. When he sleeps he sleeps in that country, yet at this point MacDonald returns the reader to the actualities of nineteenth century working class life, and a realist narrative. Reality and the imagination become fused through Diamond, for he is active in the domain of the working cabbies whilst increasingly strongly "living" in the country at the back of the north wind. The result is that the enhanced experience of Diamond increases the effect he has upon the working and social communities.

Diamond's father's working situation has changed and he decides to go into business for himself as a cab driver. Here the impact upon changes in working conditions become evident, and the emphasis moves to the self-employed, in accord with the ethos of Samuel Smiles *Book of Self Help* (1859). The responsibility falls more greatly upon the individual to effect change in their lives and on those of others. The responsibilities of Diamond's parents per se also increase with the birth of a new baby. Diamond extends great love, celebrating joy with his little brother, demonstrating a feminine caring approach. Diamond also eventually assumes the position of bread-winner for the family when he takes up the cab driving business due to his father's illness. Whilst scrupulously honest and hard working he is also a good business man, ensuring, politely, that he is paid a fair remuneration for his work (*North Wind* 178*)*. His loving, caring and socially responsible attitude is thus effective in both feminine and masculine roles. Through Diamond's meeting Mr. Raymond, a gentleman, Diamond's father becomes aware of the importance for Diamond to be taught to read. MacDonald's decision in introducing Diamond to literacy emphasises the holistic approach embedded in this novel: that dissemination of imaginative experiences is related to literature and thereby the necessity for the child to be able to read. It also illustrates the need for the adult to take responsibility for all aspects of child welfare and development. However good, loving and responsible Diamond is, his innocence needs to be accompanied by experience and knowledge which will serve him in this real world.

The shift into the living conditions of the working classes with the visit to the slum cellar dwelling of Nanny and Sal, and events of Diamond's working life take the reader into an oppositional world of violence and ugliness in comparison with the serenity, beauty and love embodied in the country at the back of the north wind. However, Diamond's influence variously enables good to out and positive change to come about, not only enacted by himself, but also by the adults who are influenced by him, especially pertinently Mr. Raymond, the rich man. Whereas in Gaskell's *Mary Barton* there is a physical as well as a social divide between the classes, in MacDonald's novel the wealthy are seen to act in a philanthropic vein, bringing relief to the poor. There is no "jealousy" extended towards the rich as with Gaskell's observation, for they willingly work together. Diamond could also be said to be the embodiment of the "deep innocence" Gaskell observed in working class people she "elbowed" in the street. Diamond's spiritual benevolence derived of his innocence, is transposed into material action, which is reminiscent of the innocent character Gluck in John Ruskin's fairy tale "King of the Golden River" (written 1841, published 1851). On taking up the agricultural management of the valley, post the changing of his brothers into black stones, Gluck puts into action a socially supportive programme. This model embodied Ruskin's ideas of a social welfare system which eventually came into actuality a century later in the Welfare State–which proves that fairy tales can "come true".

The ending of the novel with Diamond's death, however, seems to deviate from the traditional notion that fairy tales always end happily, with the young innocent protagonist triumphing and receiving great reward in this life. Through Diamond's dying MacDonald maintains the integrity of his text. He refuses to perform a magical saving and return to robust health for the child. Instead,

Diamond's death reflects the probability of child mortality conducive with the period, an experience which sadly MacDonald could attest to in his own life. By Diamond's pre-pubescent death, his innocence is preserved. There is also an implied critique of Victorian society in this sad ending, suggesting that such wealth and concentration of innocence in itself, symbolised by Diamond, has no place in the real world. Charles Kingsley transformed his chimney sweep's boy Tom into a Great Man of Science, the reader knows not how because Tom was blindfolded going 'up the back stairs'. Tom's future is predictable in this practical mode since the nineteenth century was a great time for scientific discovery, engineering and industrialisation. He is not, however, allowed to marry Ellie, merely be friends, since she is of a higher class, despite his rise in status. Kingsley's recognition of the horizon of expectation stops with class; MacDonald's with morality and humanity which can totally override class barriers, eradicating poverty, ignorance and the depravities of life. MacDonald has given some hope in demonstrating that this is to some extent possible, but complete social change was in the future, and still is, for the divide between rich and poor continues to exist in the twenty first century in the United Kingdom, despite the Welfare State. Where MacDonald gives the reader the possibility of vision is in the final line of the text: "They thought he was dead. I knew that he had gone to the back of the north wind." (*North Wind* 292) The country of the imagination is where Diamond now lives, in a state which can be no other than bliss. What the adult narrator and the reader have is this experience translated into reality by Diamond and potentially to be continued in the ways in which individuals can transpose such through their own imaginative processes. As the omniscient narrator affirms, the back of the North Wind does exist, and certainly is not nonsense.

Works Cited

Carroll, Lewis. *Alice's Adventures in Wonderland and Through the Looking-Glass*. Ed. Roger Lancelyn Green, (ed.). Oxford: Oxford University Press, 1982.
Disraeli, Benjamin. *Sybil or the Two Nations*. Oxford: Oxford University Press, 1926.
Gaskell, Elizabeth. *Mary Barton*. Oxford: Oxford University Press, 1987.
Kingsley, Charles. *The Water-Babies*. Oxford: Oxford University Press, 1995.
MacDonald, George. *At the Back of the North Wind*. In *George Macdonald*. London: Octopus Books Ltd, 1979. 5-292.
"The Fantastic Imagination." *The Complete Fairy Tales*. Ed. U.C.Knoepflmacher. London: Penguin Books, 1999. 1-14.
T.S. Eliot. *T.S. Eliot Selected Poems*. London: Faber and Faber, 1954.

[i] Frederick Engels *The condition of the working class in England : from personal observation and authentic sources.* First published in Great Britain in 1892, Granada, 1969

[ii] See for example Jean Webb 'Alice as Subject in the Logic of Wonderland.' Cogan Thacker, Deborah and Webb, Jean (2002) *Introducing Children's Literature: Romanticism to Postmodernism*, London, Routledge.

[iii] Thanks to Dr. Catherine Neale, University of Worcester, for this translation.

Chapter Three

"A Sort of a Fairy Tale":
Narrative and Genre in George MacDonald's *Little Daylight*

Rachel Johnson

Introduction

George MacDonald's tale "Little Daylight*"* first appeared as Chapter 28 of his longer story *At the Back of the North Wind* (1870). It has subsequently been reprinted in other collections of fairy tales and has more recently been retold in a picture book in which the narrative is equally in the verbal and written text[iv]. I will begin this discussion by placing "Little Daylight" within the wider context of *At the Back of the North Wind* before examining the structure, motifs and characterisation within the tale with references to episodes within *At The Back Of The North Wind*. In the final section I will draw together analysis and comment made in order to identify genres represented in the tale.

The scene for "Little Daylight" is set at the close of chapter 27 of *At the Back of the North Wind* where the author as narrator takes over from the internal narrator, Mr Raymond, and provides a brief gloss on Mr Raymond's story told to children in the Children's Hospital. I will assume some reader familiarity with *At the Back of the North Wind* and the main human character Diamond. Nanny, a crossing sweeper and a friend of Diamond is recovering from her illness. Diamond had enlisted the help of Mr Raymond in order to get her into the hospital, thereby saving her life. In two sentences towards the end of the chapter, MacDonald sums up part of his essay on fairy tale from *A Dish of Orts* when he writes,

> I don't quite know how much there was in it (i.e. the tale *"Little Daylight"*) to be understood, for in such a story everyone has just to take what he can get.
> (*A Dish of Orts 257*)

"A Sort of a Fairy Tale": Narrative and Genre
in George MacDonald's *Little Daylight*

Adrian Gunther points out that the above comment, followed by the observation "they (i.e. the children) all listened with apparent satisfaction, and certainly with great attention," (257) indicates that the story's impact will be on the subconscious and on the imagination rather than on the intellect, like the poem Diamond's mother read to him previously when they were on the beach and Diamond himself was recovering from illness. The rhymes he subsequently made to soothe his baby brother operate on the imaginative and subconscious levels, rather than the intellectual, although these rhymes are concerned with rhythm in a musical rather than in a verbal sense. Both of these narratorial comments apply to the wider context of *"Little Daylight"*, that is to *At the Back of the North Wind*, as well as to the tale itself. In his introduction to the tale, the external narrator steps outside of the text as he makes the intertextual comment drawing the reader's attention to the inspiration of "The Sleeping Beauty" as a possible source for the central idea of Mr Raymond's story. By referring to "The Sleeping Beauty" the external narrator indicates the genre of 'fairy tale' to the listener, creating an expectation that what he is about to hear will follow the traditional narrative pattern of fairy tale. The external narrator also infers the expectation of change in oral storytelling when he writes "for a good storyteller tries to make his stories better every time he tells them." (257)

He embeds the idea of the genre 'fairy tale' in the mind of the listener/reader, despite the earlier comment by Mr Raymond that he will tell "a sort of a fairy one" (250) in response to the request for a fairy tale, which, incidentally, came from a little boy. The request for a true story came from a little girl. These responses in themselves indicate an inversion of the expected gender stereotypical preference in answer to the question "What sort of story shall it be?" Mr Raymond's reply "I suppose, as there is a difference, I may choose" implies an acceptance of the difference between a true story and a fairy tale, though the phrase "as there is a difference" plants a doubt as to whether that difference might not be as clear or as obvious as the requester assumed. The reader/listener expectation from any genre is culturally learned and therefore it is more difficult for him to categorise a narrative when the expected generic pattern is subverted.

At this point a summary of the tale "Little Daylight" may be helpful to ensure familiarity for the following discussion which focuses on elements of the tale.

The Princess Daylight is born to a king and queen who live in a palace with a wood on one side of it. Seven good fairies and one wicked fairy attend her christening. When the fairies confer their gifts, two out of the seven good fairies are "kept in reserve" until after the wicked fairy had done her bit, in order to "undo as much as they might" (282). The wicked fairy's curse was that the Little Daylight shall sleep all day and her physical and emotional state shall wax and wane with the moon. The best that the two remaining good fairies could do to mitigate the curse was to enable her to wake all night and provide a condition to the curse, that it should only last "until a prince comes who shall kiss her without knowing it". (282) The royal household adjusted its routine accordingly. The Princess Daylight sought solitude in the wood where she grew ever more beautiful as the moon waxed, however, as the moon waned so did her beauty.

A prince, dressed as a peasant and fleeing insurrection in his own kingdom, finds himself at the cottage of one of the good fairies. Lost in the wood at night, he discovers Daylight dancing in an open glade. With a little help from the good fairy, and from the wicked fairy, though she thought she was hindering their meeting, the prince finds Daylight again when the moon is at its weakest. She appears old and ill. The prince kisses her out of compassion for her desperate condition as he tries to ease her suffering, thinking she is about to die. He does not of course know who she is. The story ends as dawn breaks over the wood and Daylight watches the sun rise for the first time. The spell is broken.

The Wood

Having raised the listeners' expectation of a fairy tale, the narrator begins the story by setting the scene:

"On one side of every palace there must be a wood." (278)

The first sentence provides two expected fairy tale motifs, the palace and the wood, the one "open to the sun and wind", the other "growing wilder and wilder, until some wild beasts did what they liked in it." (278)

The opposition between palace and wood is the first in a series of oppositions which are interwoven throughout the story. These oppositions are indicative of Roland Barthes symbolic code in which he states that oppositions mark out the province of antithesis. In Barthes' statement that meaning can be articulated by representing its difference, the plight of Daylight as cursed never to see the sun, is delineated against the description of her appearance, which is always described in terms of sunshine, blue sky and summer, in which the daylight hours are longer.

In Northrop Frye's discussion of fictional mode he states that the typical setting for romance is a Forest (Frye 36). Though Daylight's wood is consistently referred to as a 'wood', the description of its extent and inhabitants satisfy the requirements of a forest, such as wildness, the unknown (fairies), wild beasts and ultimately, the unexplored, "nobody had ever yet got to the end of it." (278) Whilst it is clearly stated that this narrative is a fairy tale, Frye's explanation of the combining of fictional forms, one meaning of which can refer to genres, has been demonstrated at the beginning of a narrative viewed as a fairy tale by both editors and critics, [v] though the author paved the way for this flexibility by referring to the story as "a sort of a fairy one." (258) In the mixing of genre, the tale reflects in a minor way the major combination of fantasy and realism in *At the Back of the North Wind* of which it is a part.

The reference to Barthes symbolic code in connection with binary opposition invites a symbolic meaning for the wood, which, described as "trim and nice" near the palace and getting progressively wilder and uncomprehended the further from civilization it stretches, is interpreted by Gunther (Gunther 109) as representing the subconscious mind which Daylight explores more deeply as she grows older and as her physical and emotional conditions change.

At the beginning of the tale, the attention given to the wood indicates its prominence as the scene of action. As a fairy tale motif, the wood or forest is an essential part of the background. The emphasis given to it in the opening paragraph of the tale reinforces the self-conscious inclusion of the expected motifs of a fairy tale.

Daylight "made her appearance"

The birth of Little Daylight is announced against a background of a description of the elements

> when the wind and the sun were out together ... she made her appearance from somewhere (279)

The statement that "she made her appearance from somewhere" equates her looks and character with the sun and the wind and establishes the basis for her elemental, mysterious presence in the wood later in the story. The "bright eyes" and "lively ways" associated with her name, Daylight, and implying daylight as her natural element provide the second opposition, that of day and night, or light and darkness. The contrast between her looks and her enforced place of waking existence prepares the listener for the same startling discrepancy as she dances in the moonlight at night and, in her weakened state at the waning of the moon, when her hair remained "the sunniest" and her eyes a "heavenly blue, brilliant ... as the sky of a June day" giving her an "unnatural appearance." (284/5)

The Fairies

The fairies are introduced through their connection with the wood and as part of the natural world, world linking them to Daylight's elemental character. They live in trees "one, a hollow oak; another, a birch tree ..." (279). By characterising them as elementally connected to their environment the narrator has deviated from the convention of fairy tale in two ways. The first is by placing them in the history of the country:

> fairies live so much longer than we, that they can have business with a good many generations of human mortals. (279)

The second is by drawing into the story the image of the dryad from Greek mythology. The inclusion of a mythical element is another example of the "the co-existence between several generic modes" (Jameson 141). The image of the dryad is usually associated with youth, so the depiction of them as ageless not only links them to the youthfulness of Daylight, but with the ageless wise woman of, for example MacDonald's tales *The Golden Key, The Wise Woman, The Princess and the Goblin and The Princess and Curdie*. It also sets up the third opposition, that of youth and age, in preparation for the contrast between Daylight's condition and appearance at the waxing and waning of the moon.

> The more beautiful she was in the full moon, the more withered and worn did she become as the moon waned ..... she looked, ... Like an old woman exhausted with suffering. (MacDonald 283)

The wicked fairy is only referred to in terms of age and is defined by mud and swamp, parts of the natural world which were associated in the Victorian mind with ill-health and disease. [vi] The remote, unexplored place where she lived and the description of mud and swamp also equate with those parts of the British Empire associated with disease, ignorance and spiritual darkness.

The Christening

The occasion of the christening, the invitations and who is forgotten are described in a similar way to the same event in MacDonald's *Light Princess* (1867). The fairy tale convention of the christening and giving of gifts by fairies is foregrounded by the narrator's commentary on narrative expectation when he says:

> In all history we find that fairies give their remarkable gifts to prince or princess, ..., always at the christening. (260)

This assertion draws in the fourth opposition, that of goodness and wickedness as he continues: "wicked fairies choose the same time to do unkind things." (260)

The narrator's commentary continues as he introduces a brief theology of suffering into the tale.

> But I never knew of any interference on the part of a wicked fairy that did not turn out a good thing in the end. (260)

He immediately lightens the allusion by giving "Sleeping Beauty", from which "Little Daylight" is stated to be derived, as a proven example of such interference and its benefit, that is, that Sleeping Beauty was spared the "plague of young men" and woke up "when the right prince kissed her." (260)
The narrator concludes:

> For my part I cannot help wishing a good many girls would sleep until just the same fate overtook them. It would be happier for them, and more agreeable for their friends. (260)

This of course is debatable, not only in terms of the maturation process, male dominance and female independence, but also if the original Grimm's version of Sleeping Beauty is considered as the point of departure. That, however, is another discussion.

In the context of "Little Daylight", the brief interpolation of theology echoes an earlier, fuller discussion in chapters six and seven of *At the Back of the North Wind* as North Wind takes Diamond out in a storm. Her task is to sink a ship. After several pages of discussion between Diamond and North Wind as Diamond attempts to reconcile his firm belief in the goodness of North Wind with her mission to sink a ship with people on board, North Wind herself tries to explain how she hears "the sound of a far off song .. it tells me that all is right; that it is coming to swallow up all cries." (77). In the last chapter of *Phantastes*, MacDonald's first adult fantasy published in 1858, he writes:

> What we call evil, is only the best shape, which, for the person and his condition at the time, could be assumed by the best good.
> (*Phantastes 320*).

A biblical example of this line of thought can be found in Genesis 45:5, with the story of Joseph. Commentaries on MacDonald's theology[vii] discuss his theology of suffering in depth but in the present context of fairy tale it is an unexpected departure from generic convention.

The spell placed upon Daylight, despite the best efforts of the two good fairies 'kept in reserve', meant that she would not know what daylight was, would fall asleep as soon as the sun appeared and, though awake at night, would wax and wane with the moon. The rearrangement of the household to accommodate this pattern is glossed over, except for the effect of the waning moon on the princess.

> She was wan and withered like the poorest, sickliest child you might come upon in the streets of a great city in the arms of a homeless mother."
> (*At the Back of the North Wind* 283)

This is the very condition of Nanny when Diamond found her ill and before she was brought to the children's hospital. The wider context of the fairy tale is thus foregrounded against the immediate realism of Diamond's London as presented in *At the Back of the North Wind*.

"And thus things went on until she was nearly seventeen years of age."

Seventeen was the age at which the Light Princess discovered water, just as Daylight discovered the element 'moonlight'. The Light Princess swam in the lake, Daylight danced in the moonlight. In this way, both gained independence and freedom. Gunther writes:

> the active agent in his (MacDonald's) fairy tales is almost always female. (Gunther 111)

She contrasts Daylight with the passive heroine of traditional tales, particularly Sleeping Beauty. Her view ignores both the high proportion of traditional fairy tale heroines who are the propelling force of the tale and the unavoidable fact that Daylight still has to await her prince before she can be freed from the spell which binds her to an unbalanced life in which the sun does not feature. She can only experience the reflection of the source of light and enjoy the moon.

Enter the Prince

It is as Daylight is reaching "the zenith of her loveliness" (293) as the moon was "nearer the full", that the prince discovers her. One paragraph explains how the prince came to be deep in the wood. This paragraph reads like a potted version of a boy's adventure story and includes political rebellion, violence, flight, disguise and hardship of the kind that toughens the prince and brings out the essential "decency" and thoughtfulness of his character. The only unexpected trait is his passivity. His action is portrayed in terms of lack of choice. He was "compelled to flee for his life", (286). He did not abandon his peasant disguise because "he had no other clothes to put on and ... very little money" (286). He told no-one he was a prince, "For he felt a prince ought to be able to get on like other people." (287) and he had set out on his quest through necessity. MacDonald continues to parody the fairy tale narrative when he says of the prince:

> "He had read of princes setting out upon adventure; and here he was in similar case, only without having had a choice in the matter." (287)

The prince is following a passive destiny, but that destiny is still that of the fairy tale figure of the youngest or only son, and the outcome will depend upon an act of spontaneous compassion.

From the point of the prince's appearance, the expected fairy tale motifs gather around him. Although he does not realise it, he receives supernatural help from the good fairy and from her gifts, which he has with him just when they are needed. These gifts are the tinder box and a small bottle of cordial; both gifts that resonate with former fairy tale appearances. The hospitality of the good fairy reinforces her parallels with the wise women already cited from MacDonald's tales. The food she gives him and the rest he has in her cottage have an extra-ordinary restorative effect, just as the food and rest offered by the wise woman in *The Wise Woman, The Golden Key* and *The Princess and the Goblin* restores Rosamund, Tangle and Irene.

At the point when the prince first sees her, Daylight is living in her own house deep in the wood. As she grew older, she had retreated further into the darker, wilder parts of the wood until she settled at the edge of an open glade, "for here the full moon shone free and glorious" (266.) The prince had "wandered and wandered, and got nowhere" (268) before he reached this open glade. 'Somewhere' is defined in the prince's terms as anywhere not in the wood, so anywhere still in the wood he felt to be "nowhere". The paradox is that he reached the only place where he needed to be to fulfil his destiny. In her retreat into the wood, Daylight, still described in terms of the sun and the summer sky, was, in the process of maturation, taming the unknown, taking her daylight character into the dark unexplored recesses of the wood, even while she waned with the moon. When the prince first observed her dancing and singing in the glade, she appeared to him as "some strange being of the wood" (269), an elemental creature rather than a human being.

Daylight's dance graphically illustrates Maria Nikolajeva's concept of children's fiction as "a symbolic depiction of a maturation process" (Nikolajeva 1) in its cyclical motion and its continual movement from the circular to the linear as Daylight progresses towards the completion of her character as she approaches adulthood. She is of course unaware of this significance. Her dance is inspired by the fullness of the moon and "the exuberance of her delight"

(274). Fairy tale, romance and myth, the three genres that 'co-exist', to use Jameson's term, in this story, all exist in mythical time, emphasising the importance of the cycles of nature. In this story the cyclical nature of the phases of the moon are, at the point of the prince's entry, intersected by the linearity of his story up to the point of his meeting with Daylight. At this point of intersection he breaks into and joins her to complete the transformation of both their realities which is characteristic of both romance and fairy tale.

"The very thing she was trying to prevent" (MacDonald 278)

When the bad fairy realised the prince had "seen Daylight", she contrived by her deceitful spells, that the next night the prince could not by any endeavour find his way to the glade." (MacDonald 278) Here the narrator directly breaks into the story to reinforce the theological commentary he had inserted earlier:

> But it is all of no consequence, for what they (the wicked fairies) do never succeeds; nay, in the end it brings about the very thing they are trying to prevent ...... from the beginning of the world they have really helped instead of thwarting the good fairies. (278)

The princess, "dancing like an embodied sunbeam" (274), had already taken control of what might have been a relationship "for, however much she might desire to be set free, she was dreadfully afraid of the wrong prince." (278)

By preventing the prince from finding Daylight again until she was in her 'waned' condition, the wicked fairy ruled out any possibility of the spell being broken because she had ruled out compassion, not having any herself. As Maria Tatar writes, in fairy tales "compassion counts" (Tatar 79) and, true to the compassionate act performed by the youngest or only son in traditional fairy tales, the prince kisses the princess when she appears old and ill, purely out of compassion and without knowing that in doing this act, he is fulfilling his destiny and freeing Daylight from the spell.

The fairy tale narrative structure always includes the element of struggle, or test. The seven days and nights when the prince is wandering in the wood equates, within this structure, with the struggle, or test, a test which continues until his treatment of the supposedly old and sick woman is revealed. Searching for the princess, whom he has only seen "at the zenith of her loveliness" (MacDonald 366) his behaviour toward the person he finds at the foot of a great birch tree is entirely disinterested. It is at this point that the two gifts from the good fairy are needed; the tinderbox to light a fire and the cordial which revived the princess sufficiently for her to open her eyes and look at the prince. It is worth noting that this is the second time the princess has been found at the foot of a birch tree. One of the good fairies lived in a birch tree and may have been aiding the princess more than she realised.

The prince's compassionate kiss completes the fairy tale cycle of quest, test, success, by freeing the princess. The final expectation in a fairy tale narrative is that of success, or homecoming, which in this case does not happen. As with so many of MacDonald's stories, there is no conclusive ending. Cohan and Shires point out that the opening and closing of a story mark events paradigmatically (Cohan 66), that is, the initial event is replaced or transformed by the closing event. Though "Little Daylight" follows this pattern, it departs from the expected "happy ever after" ending and finishes with the prince and princess still in the wood facing "the first gleam of morning" (MacDonald 281). As Gunther states:

> the ending is the beginning, a new stage in the process, a new birth.
> (Gunther 116)

This returns the reader into the host story, *At the Back of the North Wind*, which ends with what appears to be the death of Diamond. The narrator, Mr. Raymond, articulates one of MacDonald's key ideas when he says "they thought he was dead. I knew he had gone to the back of the North Wind" (MacDonald 278) thereby indicating that the dimension "At the Back of the North Wind" was more real, and reaching, it was a movement into more life.

Conclusion

In this brief examination of the tale I have demonstrated how the fairy tale pattern of journey, test, success, interwoven with the romance pattern of destiny, providence, ethical opposition and transformation, encompasses the progress of the Prince and Daylight within and without their expected fairy tale roles. The "reliance on antecedents for parodic effects" (Knoepflmacher 257) is so overt as to prepare the listener for the subversion of narrative and character and the oppositions found in setting, character, characteristics, time, and ethics. The narrator leaves the Prince and Daylight as the sun rises on the next phase of their lives, just as the reader is pulled back into the hospital ward, with the words:

"The children in the hospital "were delighted" (282) with the story". Ending with the expectation that daily life in the world of the palace with its consequent responsibilities and practicalities would resume, Diamond and Mr Raymond are led back into the practicalities of their responsibility for the recovering Nanny. The tale "Little Daylight" is, therefore, a turning point in *At the Back of the North Wind* as the lives of Diamond's family, Nanny and Mr Raymond, hitherto touching only occasionally, become inextricably linked. Romance and fairy tale leak into the realistic aspects of *At the Back of the North Wind*, transforming "ordinary reality." (Jameson 110)

Works Cited

Bell, Anthea and Duntze, Dorothee (illustrator), ed. *"Little Daylight" by George MacDonald.* London: North South Books, 1987.
Cohan, Steven and Shires, Linda M. *Telling Stories: A Theoretical Analysis of Narrative Fiction.* New York and London: Routledge, 1988.
Gunther, Adrian. ""Little Daylight": An Old Tale Transfigured." *Children's Literature in Education* 26.2 (1995): 107-17.
Jameson, Fredric. *The Political Unconscious: Narrative as a Socially Symbolic Act.* Ithaca: Cornell University Press, 1981.
Knoepflmacher, U. C. *Ventures into Childhood: Victorians, Fairy Tales, and Femininity.* Chicago and London: Chicago University Press, 1998.
MacDonald, George. *At the Back of the North Wind.* Strahan & Co. 1870. Whitethorn: Johannesen, 1992.
—. *Phantastes.* Smith Elder and Co. 1858. Whitethorn: Johannesen, 1994.
Nikolajeva, Maria. *From Mythic to Linear.* Lanham, MD: Scarecrow, 2000.
Tatar, Maria. *Off with Their Heads!: Fairy Tales and the Culture of Childhood.* Princeton, NJ: Princeton University Press, 1992.
Wilson, A. N. *The Victorians.* Hutchinson 2002. London: Arrow Books, 2003.

[iv] Anthea and Duntze Bell, Dorothee (illustrator), ed., *Little Daylight by George MacDonald* (London: North South Books, 1987).
[v] See for example Sadler's *Gifts of the Child Christ* and Gunther's article referenced in the bibliography.
[vi] See information on damp, sanitation and swamp miasmas in A. N. Wilson, *The Victorians* (London: Arrow Books, 2003).
[vii] For example Hein, Raeper, Phillips.

CHAPTER FOUR

DIFFERENCES IN SIMILARITIES: *LITTLE DAYLIGHT* AND *THE LIGHT PRINCESS*

YUKO ASHITAGAWA

Introduction

In this essay I intend to offer a re-reading of George MacDonald's two relatively short narratives that have been noted for their resemblance to each other and show that they can be read as quite different texts. This will be useful in bringing to attention some of the problems that accompany assimilatory reading. Both "Little Daylight" and "The Light Princess" have been considered similar to each other as variants of the "Sleeping Beauty" tale. For example, William Raeper writes that MacDonald's 'fairy-tales draw on many traditional motifs' and that 'christenings go wrong in "Little Daylight" and "The Light Princess" as they do in "Sleeping Beauty"' (Raeper 314); according to Jack Zipes, "*The Light Princess*" (1864) like his tale "Little Daylight" (1867) is a parody of *Sleeping Beauty* and *Rapunzel*, and, for that matter, it reflects MacDonald's disrespectful attitude toward traditional folk and fairy tales' (Zipes 105); Roderick McGillis's comment on *The Princess and the Goblin* reads: "Here MacDonald acknowledges the famous story, 'Sleeping Beauty', as a source for his story. [...] He parodies the story in *The Light Princess* (1864) and *Little Daylight* (1871)" (McGillis 347); and U. C. Knoepflmacher notes that "Little Daylight" "in many ways resembles" "The Light Princess" (350) and that "The Light Princess" contains "an allusion to the christening episode in Perrault's "The Sleeping Beauty of the Woods," which MacDonald more directly travesties in the opening of "Little Daylight" (343). All the four critics discuss the two texts in relation to "Sleeping Beauty" as a "source" which these narratives "draw on" or "parody". I am not saying that these critics are wrong, but I would argue that this kind of description concerns only one particular aspect of these two texts, which have differences as well as similarities.

There are two notable points in the statements cited above. First, "Little Daylight" and "The Light Princess" are bundled together on the grounds that both are written by the same author, namely George MacDonald. This posits the author as a coherent subject that writes the texts with certain authorial intention or an "attitude". In fact, this notion of the author forms the basis of most "MacDonald studies" (including this volume of essays). The second point is that both "The Light Princess" and "Little Daylight" are assumed to belong to the same genre and associated with a particular "source" text. The narratives are analysed in terms of how they follow or depart from the fairy-tale tradition of "Sleeping Beauty". These ways of reading will be questioned by the differences I point out between the two texts, for the differences can demonstrate that potentially contradictory ideas can be read in the two texts and that the generic classification of the texts as fairy tales does not say much about some important characteristics of the texts. Among many dissimilarities that can be read between "Little Daylight" and "The Light Princess", this essay focuses on how the ideas of knowledge in relation to the world and language are constructed differently in both texts.

The Christening Episodes

It is true that both "Little Daylight" and "The Light Princess" can be summarised as narratives in which a bewitched princess is saved by a prince; however, there are many other issues that the two texts present. For a start, let us compare the two narratives' christening episodes which are mentioned by Raeper and Knoepflmacher. Although both christenings may "go wrong" as Raeper puts it, the texts differ from each other in a way that is consistent with what I will discuss later in more detail. There are reasons why the christenings go wrong: someone fails to be invited. "Little Daylight" narrates the circumstances thus: "Of course all the known fairies were invited to the christening. But the king and queen never thought of inviting an old witch. For the power of the fairies they have by nature; whereas a witch gets her power by wickedness" ("Little Daylight" 150). The passage is concerned with distinguishing between fairies and witches by the source of their "power", although to be precise, the "fairies" are plural while the "witch" is singular. This seems to suggest that there are not as many witches as fairies, though both have some kind of power that is either inherent or acquired. "Nature" is contrasted with "wickedness", which is implied to be unnatural and worthy of disapproval. There is an idea of a law: good fairies are "of course" invited to the christening, but if your power is not natural, you are a wicked witch and will never be invited. The king and queen, who know the distinction, are justified in ignoring the witch. It is wicked to go against nature, which clearly defines fairies as well as witches.

On the other hand, the narration of "The Light Princess" is interested in a different matter:

> The day drew near when the infant must be christened. The king wrote all the invitations with his own hand. Of course somebody was forgotten.
> Now it does not generally matter if somebody *is* forgotten, only you must mind who. Unfortunately, the king forgot without intending to forget; and so the chance fell upon the Princess Makemnoit, which was awkward. (16)

This claims that forgetting someone for a christening is a matter of course, and goes on to comment on the act of forgetting. Forgetting itself is not problematic unless it involves someone who creates an "awkward" situation. There are different ways of forgetting: the expression that the king forgets "without intending to forget" implies the other possibility of forgetting with intention. To avoid the awkwardness, either the king should have been careful in choosing whom to forget, or the "chance" should have fallen on someone else. The passage shows an interest in language by bringing up different meanings of forgetting. It also highlights the relationship among sound, spelling and meaning, with the name "Makemnoit" that could be pronounced as "make-'em-know-it". This draws attention to the process of reading or understanding of language.

In both narratives, the uninvited woman turns up at the christening. "Little Daylight" explains why she comes:

> Of course the old hag was there without being asked. Not to be asked was just what she wanted, that she might have a sort of a reason for doing what she wished to do. For somehow even the wickedest of creatures likes a pretext for doing the wrong thing. (150).

Another law is introduced, which concerns "a sort of a reason" for doing what one wishes to do. Even the "wickedest of creatures" that wants to do wrong things anyway likes to obey the law of causality. The narration establishes that this is all predictable: the old woman's presence is as taken for granted as the fact that she is not invited. Meanwhile, Princess Makemnoit, that is the light princess's aunt, comes for a slightly different reason:

> She despised all the modes we read of in history, in which offended fairies and witches have taken their revenges; and therefore, after waiting and waiting in vain for an invitation, she made up her mind at last to go without one, and make the whole family miserable, like a princess as she was. (16).

What the Princess Makemnoit, who is a "witch" herself, models herself on is the "history" of fairies and witches, which "we" are supposed to be familiar with. Makemnoit "despise[s]" the tradition, and "therefore" decides to go to the christening, which seems to mean that in her view all those "modes" are not grand enough and not suitable for a princess like her. There are traditional modes of revenge, but they are claimed to be different from this particular witch's. She does not necessarily want to do wrong things from the first, but she is "offended" at being forgotten and has to have her revenge. The king's careless "forgetting" leads to this consequence.

What happens at the christening also has dissimilar characteristics in the two narratives. After five fairies have given their gifts to the child, the "wicked fairy" of "Little Daylight" asks the archbishop to repeat the princess's name:

> "With pleasure, my good woman," said the archbishop, stooping to shout in her ear: "the infant's name is little Daylight."
> "And little daylight it shall be," cried the fairy, in the tone of a dry axle, "and little good shall any of her gifts do her. For I bestow upon her the gift of sleeping all day long, whether she will or not. Ha, ha! He, he! Hi, hi!" (151)

It is interesting to note that despite the previously made distinction between fairies and witches, this uninvited guest is called a "fairy". She seems to be part of the natural order though she is often called a "wicked" one. She is like a machine that plays a limited role, her voice being withered and mechanical in the manner of a "dry axle". The passage also draws attention to the distinction between a proper noun and an ordinary noun, along with different uses of the word "little" as an adjective or an adverb. The relationship between words and things are foregrounded. First there is a thing or the baby whose name is announced; then the wicked fairy gives her a "gift" that suits the name. The words, "little" and "Daylight / daylight", connect the princess and the gift. In a way the gift is predetermined by the princess's name, which appears in the text before the christening scene. In the opening paragraph of the narrative, the name is already mentioned: "there was a very grand wood indeed beside the palace of the king who was going to be Daylight's father" (149). This is the first time she is referred to, and she is called by her proper name rather than by a general noun like a baby or a princess. Little Daylight has an identity as "Daylight", and the fairy's magic does not entirely alter it.

"The Light Princess" does not have other fairies who try to protect the baby princess, nor does the witch talk to the other people around. She throws something into the water and keeps quiet till the water is applied to the baby's face:

But at that moment she turned round in her place three times, and muttered the following words, loud enough for those beside her to hear:
Light of spirit, by my charms,
   Light of body, every part,
Never weary human arms—
   Only crush thy parents' heart!
They all thought she had lost her wits, and was repeating some foolish nursery rhyme; but a shudder went through the whole of them notwithstanding. The baby, on the contrary, began to laugh and crow [...]
The mischief was done. (17)

The "mischief" is done through the combination of some material, action, and words. It is not clear why the witch chooses to make the baby "light", other than the likelihood that it will handicap the princess and "crush" her parents' heart. The princess's name is not mentioned throughout the narrative. To some extent the witch's choice is arbitrary, though this does not affect the magic's power. The words of the "charms" are only heard by "those beside her" but have an immediate effect on the baby. The words are the announcement of what the witch is trying to make happen and at the same time the enactment of her charms. The verse distinguishes between "spirit" and "body" but connects them by saying that both are "light" in the princess, thus depriving her of gravity. It also tells of its effects on the people: while no "human arms" feel the weight of the baby, only her parents feel the weight in their heart. The verse indeed produces different reactions: the baby acts "contrary" to everyone else, looking happy when the others are not. The verse directly calls to the princess as "thou"; to other people it sounds like a "foolish" but sinister nursery rhyme.

Although both christening episodes contain an uninvited guest's interference, they show different details and tendencies. These are related to the worldview of each text, as we shall see next.

"Little Daylight": The World as Substance

In my reading, "Little Daylight" presents the world as substance that exists independently of language. Language here can be a medium that conveys part of the world as some kind of truth or reality. Consequently knowledge is something to be acquired directly through experience or indirectly through language, and one either knows or does not know. This explains why the distinction between knowing and not knowing is an important issue in this text. Fulfilment of the prophecy depends on the prince's not knowing it, and Princess Daylight cannot know the sun until then. The following quotation is from the end of the christening scene, when it is proclaimed by the wicked fairy that

Princess Daylight has to sleep all day and wake all night, and "wax and wane" with the moon:

> But out stepped another fairy, for they had been wise enough to keep two in reserve, because every fairy knew the trick of one.
> "Until," said the seventh fairy, "a prince comes who shall kiss her without knowing it." [...]
> "I don't know what that means," said the poor king to the seventh fairy.
> "Don't be afraid. The meaning will come with the thing itself," said she. (151-52)

The distinction between knowing and not knowing is highlighted. The knowledge of the good fairies saves the princess: they are "wise enough", knowing the trick of the wicked fairy. The seventh fairy's prophecy requires a prince's non-knowledge. The king comments that he does not know what that means, to which the seventh fairy replies that he will know eventually. She seems to know but would not tell. The king does not attempt to interpret the prophecy, since "the meaning" at that moment is not accessible to him: there is only one right meaning, and if he cannot get it now, he does not know. The "meaning" and the "thing itself" are differentiated, though they are supposed to "come" together. The implication is that language as a medium is meaningless and useless unless it is accompanied by the "thing itself", that is to say, something substantial.

A similar idea is presented in a conversation between Princess Daylight and the prince:

> "Can you tell me what the sun is like?" she asked.
> "No," he answered. "But where's the good of asking what you know?"
> "But I don't know," she rejoined.
> "Why, everybody knows."
> "That's the very thing: I'm not everybody. I've never seen the sun."
> "Then you can't know what it's like till you do see it." (159)

The prince cannot tell what the sun is like, nor does he think telling will make the princess know it. The world is solid and pre-existent, and language here is inadequate to the task of representing the world. Although later the prince is compelled to answer the princess's questions about the sun and describes it in comparison with such things as the lightning and the moon, they both know that the words cannot substitute the thing itself. What the princess, who does not know the sun, knows is that she will never have the proper knowledge about the sun till she actually sees it. She also knows when someone is telling the truth, as the conversation continues:

"I think you must be a prince," said the princess.
"Do I look like one?" said the prince.
"I can't quite say that."
"Then why do you think so?"
"Because you both do what you are told and speak the truth." (159)

She thinks that he must be a prince because of what he does and what he says rather than his appearance. Both the prince and the princess share the premise that the essential thing is the "truth", which is recognisable to those who know. The "truth" is a kind of law that governs the world, whether or not one is aware of it.

On the other hand, knowledge in this narrative can also be acquired through words to some extent. The prince has learnt about some other princes: "He had read of princes setting out upon adventure; and here he was out in similar case, only without having had a choice in the matter. He would go on, and see what would come of it" (154). He compares himself with other standard princes in books and notes his similarity and difference to them. Nevertheless, the books do not show him what is going to happen to him. He has to find that out in person. He gains help from a good fairy, who refuses to tell "secrets" to him. Some things must be hidden from this prince; telling will reveal it. In this case, the idea is that certain parts of the world can be accessible through language. While this seems to assume a stronger power of language than what I have read in the examples above, the basic worldview is consistent: whatever language does, it does not affect the status of the world as pre-existent and substantial. The world is independent of language, which may or may not be able to represent the world. In effect, however, language does not give much information to the prince, because the good fairy does not allow it to. The point of "secrets" is to suggest that there are things one cannot know. The princess, too, checks herself when she mentions the prophecy, saying "And I never shall wake until—" (160) and walks away. The prince may know that there are important issues concerning the princess, but he ought not be told what they are.

Like the characters, the narration is also interested in knowing and not knowing. The narrator comments thus on christening curses:

> But I never knew of any interference on the part of a wicked fairy that did not turn out a good thing in the end. What a good thing, for instance, it was that one princess should sleep for a hundred years! Was she not saved from all the plague of young men who were not worthy of her? And did she not come awake exactly at the right moment when the right prince kissed her? (150)

The narrator claims an authority on the matter: he or she knows that a wicked fairy's interference will bring about a good result. The comments on the princess, who is likely to be the one known as the Sleeping Beauty, are based on the idea that there are "worthy" and "right" things as well as unworthy and wrong things. All goes well in the world where a wicked thing only helps the good. The narrator then continues: "For my part, I cannot help wishing a good many girls would sleep till just the same fate overtook them. It would be happier for them, and more agreeable to their friends" (150). The princess in the past is contrasted with "a good many girls" in the present. The narrator implies that many girls are not as fortunate as princesses who come across wicked fairies. In other words, things that are conventional in fairy stories just do not happen to the majority of ordinary people. Just as language is not the "thing itself", life is not like a fairy tale.

The narrator emphasises the fact that most of the time he or she knows more than any character in the narrative. The wicked fairy as well as the prince does not know what "we" and the good fairy know, namely what has happened to wicked fairies and what is going to happen. When the prince first meets the good fairy, "The moment she saw him she knew quite well who he was and what was going to come of it; but she was not at liberty to interfere with the orderly march of events" (154). The good fairy lets the "orderly march of events" to proceed, though—or because—she knows what is going to happen. Goodness thus resides in what is natural and orderly, with which wickedness tries to interfere. The narrator points out that wicked fairies never win, even though they seem to have the advantage over the good in that they are not "bound by the laws which the good fairies obey":

> So you see that somehow, for all their cleverness, wicked fairies are dreadfully stupid, for, although from the beginning of the world they have really helped instead of thwarting the good fairies, not one of them is a bit the wiser for it. She will try the bad thing just as they all did before her; and succeeds no better of course. (161)

A fairy-tale tradition is made explicit and followed; the course of the narrative is predictable. The wickedness, or rather stupidity, of the wicked fairies benefits the good. That is to say, the world has its own law and order whether one knows it or not, and seeming reversal or transgression is still part of that law and order. This can explain why the wicked fairy is left unpunished in the narrative.

The world in "Little Daylight" follows a consistent law, which supports the natural and essential. The wicked fairy's magic does not affect a fundamental part of the princess in the first place: "For at certain seasons the palace rang all night with bursts of laughter from little Daylight, whose heart the old fairy's curse could not reach; she was Daylight still, only a little in the wrong place [...]" (152). The "heart" or the essence of Daylight is intact. Her nature is kept from the first and she is regarded as a young, beautiful princess: "As she grew older she had grown more and more beautiful, with the sunniest hair and the loveliest eyes [...]. But so much more painful and sad was the change as her bad time came on. [...] This was the more painful that her appearance was unnatural; for her hair and eyes did not change" (153). She is basically beautiful, and the "change" into the "unnatural" appearance of an old woman comes at her "bad time". Interestingly, the unnaturalness at her bad time results from the fact that her hair and eyes are kept "natural" in the sense that they are what she is born with while the other parts are changed. Naturalness here implies the notion of harmony, which the princess regains in the end.

The "wicked" and the "bad" are ignorant of the fact that they are helping the enemy. Their situation is quite similar to that of the prince, who has to save the princess unknowingly. The narrator in fact refers to the prince's ignorance: "It would take me too long to tell her tricks. They would be amusing to us, who know that they could not do any harm, but they were something other than amusing to the poor prince" (162). The narrator contrasts "us" with the prince and draws attention not only to the different amount of knowledge but also to the difference in position: "we" are looking at the prince from a safe place outside of his story. At the same time the narrator suggests that the narratee is not told everything, claiming that for the sake of brevity, details of "her tricks" are omitted. The text presents the world as a knowable substance that may or may not be conveyed through language, and the narrator is the one that knows best.

"The Light Princess": The World as Text

In "The Light Princess", the world is a text that is subject to interpretation: in a sense language constitutes reality, and appearance is all there is to be interpreted. Thus the witch's magical words have an immediate effect on the baby princess, and punning, to which this text often draws attention, is not just a word-play but substantial: the princess is "light" of both mind and body, being deprived of "gravity". Another example of punning foregrounds the ways the characters constantly interpret one another, displaying the textuality of the world. The king is having an argument with the queen, whose remark annoys him:

> But it was not this reflection on his hair that arrested him; it was the double use of the word *light*. For the king hated all witticisms, and punning especially. And besides, he could not tell whether the queen meant light-*haired* or light-*heired*; for why might she not aspirate her vowels when she was ex-asperated herself? (21)

It is not the word itself but how it is used with which the king is concerned. Language is not stable here. It does not matter what the queen meant, since the king reacts according to his interpretation of her words. Exasperation may cause aspiration of vowels; this entails the idea that language may be a manifestation of emotion. To put it another way, emotion is interpreted as language. The passage is narrated from the king's perspective, and ends in a mixture of direct quotation and reported thoughts. The narration is "half inside" the king and is interested in how language works.

"The Light Princess" presents the idea that one cannot fully control language. The king hates punning, saying: "duplicity of any sort is exceedingly objectionable between married people of any rank, not to say kings and queens; and the most objectionable form duplicity can assume is that of punning" (22); yet he himself cannot escape the "duplicity". For one thing, the word "duplicity" in this case cannot be limited to a single, stable use or meaning, but can be taken to mean both doubleness and deceit. The irony is that the king is not aware of his own "duplicity", as another example illustrates: the king "requested them to consult together as to what might be the cause and probable cure of her *infirmity*. The king laid stress upon the word, but failed to discover his own pun" (26). Here the princess's illness amounts to her lightness, and the king refers to both in one word without knowing it. Even those who resent language's ambiguity are not free of it.

The world being a text does not mean that there is no notion of rules or standards. There are ideas of the normal and natural, though they are not absolute or unified. The princess loves water, and the narration proceeds: "The root of this preference no doubt, although the princess did not recognise it as such, was, that the moment she got into it, she recovered the natural right of which she had been so wickedly deprived—namely, gravity" (28). The narrator has "no doubt" and knows more than the princess about the reason why she loves water. Gravity is the princess's "natural right", as she was born with it and had it until she was bewitched at the christening. The princess's "light" condition is described to be not normal, as in "it would be endless to relate all the odd incidents resulting from this peculiarity of the young princess" (19-20). The narrator claims to have more examples than can be related, emphasising that the princess is peculiar and causes "odd" things in contrast with the ordinary. However, unlike Daylight, the light princess herself does not wish to be delivered from the witch's spell except when she thinks of the easiness of getting into water with gravity. To her the lightness is most of the time normal, as she says: "I have a curious feeling sometimes, as if I were the only person that had any sense in the whole world" (25). She is aware of her difference from other people, but does not necessarily see herself as odd or abnormal.

This world also has laws and things do not happen at random. Nevertheless, these laws are not indestructible. The narrator comments on Princess Makemnoit's magic:

> Her atrocious aunt had deprived the child of all her gravity. If you ask me how this was effected, I answer, 'In the easiest way in the world. She had only to destroy gravitation.' For the princess was a philosopher, and knew all the *ins* and *outs* of the laws of gravitation as well as the *ins* and *outs* of her boot-lace. And being a witch as well, she could abrogate those laws in a moment; or at least so clog their wheels and rust their bearings, that they would not work at all. But we have more to do with what followed than with how it was done. (17)

A philosopher has knowledge, and a witch has power. The "laws of gravitation", which are discussed on the same level as a "boot-lace", are like machines, with their "wheels" and "bearings". The laws of the world can be bent: gravitation can be destroyed, or "at least" can be stopped. The rephrasing signals the carefulness with words of the narrator, who is here having a hypothetical conversation with the audience as "you" before moving into the more inclusive "we". In this narrative the course of events is unpredictable, and following the consequence is said to be more important than contemplating the cause. As a result of the destruction of gravitation, the light princess's condition is beyond the laws of nature: "Indeed, the most complete knowledge of the laws of nature would have been unserviceable in her case; for it was impossible to classify her. She was a fifth imponderable body, sharing all the other properties of the ponderable" (28). The laws of nature and the knowledge of them have limits, and one can go beyond. Nonetheless, by saying that it was impossible to classify her, the narration of course classifies the princess as the unclassifiable and as a "fifth imponderable body". She is still interpreted within language, in so far as the princess exists in that world.

In this world laws may be surpassed and the fate is not guaranteed, though the course of narrative may turn out to follow a certain path through which troubles are undone. The world may have its own logic of progression, as the discovery of the gold-plate oracle that leads to the cure of the princess suggests, but this idea is not authorised as such by the narration. The plate has an "enigmatical" poem on one side and some sentences that "explained it a little" (43) on the other, thus offering a key to the interpretation but not directly providing definite information. Unlike the people in "Little Daylight" that wait for the orderly march of events, the characters in "The Light Princess" are not promised a happy ending, for the plate says: "If the nation could not provide one hero, it was time it should perish" (44). The prince has to make up his mind whether to do what the oracle seems to say. In the end, he tries and succeeds in collaboration with the princess, and the "atrocious" witch is dead so that there will be no further threat. The world is something that the characters have to make to some degree, although they are also part of the world.

In this textual world, what matters is the ability to understand and interpret rather than being accessible to truth. Knowledge is reading or interpretation, and it is not just words that are subject to interpretation. The prince "reads" the princess:

> "Will you be in the lake to-morrow night?" the prince ventured to ask.
> "To be sure I will. I don't think so. Perhaps," was the princess's somewhat strange answer.
> But the prince was intelligent enough not to press her further; and merely whispered, as he gave her the parting lift,
> "Don't tell." The only answer the princess returned was a roguish look. [...] The look seemed to say, "Never fear. It is too good fun to spoil that way." (35)

The princess's "somewhat strange" answer seems to be saying three different things, but the prince interprets the answer as a signal that the princess does not want to make an assertion. He is "intelligent enough" to be able to produce an interpretation by himself, not only of words but also of the princess's "roguish look". The look is a kind of language and in fact is translated into words here. The narration at the end is in the prince's perspective, reporting what her look "seemed" to him to say but not authorising this interpretation. One can only interpret things according to one's ability. The prince asks the princess not to "tell" anybody, since even if language is not a transparent medium, it can still mean something.

The prince is a good reader, and the princess can be good, too. Like Princess Daylight, the light princess also knows that the prince is a prince, but not for the same reason. At their second meeting, the princess calls him "prince" even though he has not told her who he is. The prince asks her how she knows he is a prince, to which she replies: "Because you are a very nice young man, prince" (38). Her judgement is based on his appearance and behaviour, and she does not mention the "truth" as did Daylight. The definition of a prince for the light princess does not involve universal truth; implicitly any "very nice young man" can be read as a prince to her. However, there are things which her "lightness" does not allow her to interpret or understand. Her cure does not depend on what is hidden from her but on what she cannot understand:

> But when the prince, who had really fallen in love when he fell in the lake, began to talk to her about love, she always turned her head towards him and laughed. After a while she began to look puzzled, as if she were trying to understand what he meant, but could not—revealing a notion that he meant something. (38-39)

The prince falls in love as well as in the lake, which displays another example of the "duplicity" of language. His talk of love is uninterpretable to the princess; she does not share his ways of thinking. Though she seems to be aware that the prince means something, she cannot understand it despite her effort. She may appear to be in a similar situation to Daylight's father when he heard the prophecy, but here the concern is with understanding rather than knowing: it is not lack of information that prevents her understanding but lack of certain ability. Moreover, to be precise, all this seems so, because her reaction here is narrated from the prince's perspective. Her look is interpreted as one of puzzlement. The text thus foregrounds the way the characters constantly read each other. Throughout the story, narrative perspective moves around and seems less stable than in "Little Daylight". This augments the relative fragmentariness of "The Light Princess", which is divided into titled sections whereas "Little Daylight" is not. The fragmentariness indicates that "The Light Princess" is not concerned with a universal truth but with particular standpoints.

The characters do not have a unified view of the world. In most of the narrative, the prince and the princess do not share the same thoughts about love, nor does the princess think much of gravity as others do. Knowledge of the world is not uniform or complete since it is interpretation and subject to perspective, as the disagreement between the two philosophers illustrates: "Their consultation consisted chiefly in propounding and supporting, for the thousandth time, each his favourite theories" (26). Both have "favourite theories" about the world, which are incompatible but which each believes to be right. In a way each lives in as well as is created by his own world, for these philosophers have different personalities: "Hum-Drum was a Materialist, and Kopy-Keck was a Spiritualist. The former was slow and sententious; the latter was quick and flighty: the latter had generally the first word; the former the last" (27). Hum-Drum has the characteristics of what he defines as a material, and Kopy-Keck is like a spirit in his theory. They are at the head of the "college of Metaphysicians" and described as "two very wise Chinese philosophers" (26), but they are not "wise enough" (30) to restore the princess's gravity even when they have agreed on something. They act on a different principle from the king's, which is also different from that of the princess or the prince.

Meanings can be different to different people. Words and ideas do not have rigid one-to-one correspondence in this narrative. The prince reasons himself, considering what "life" means to him: "She will die if I don't do it, and life would be nothing to me without her; so I shall lose nothing by doing it" (44). For him, the princess is a necessary condition of life. Though it is first referred to as "life", it is "nothing" if it lacks the princess. Meaning can also shift, as when the prince redefines "gravity" for the princess after she has regained it:

"Is this the gravity you used to make so much of?" said she one day to the prince, as he raised her from the floor. "For my part, I was a great deal more comfortable without it."

"No, no, that's not it. This is it," replied the prince, as he took her up, and carried her about like a baby, kissing her all the time. "This is gravity."

"That's better," said she. "I don't mind that so much."

[…]. I fear she complained of her gravity more than once after this, notwithstanding. (52)

First the gravity is a nuisance that makes her tumble on the floor; then it involves being lovingly carried around and kissed; afterwards it often returns to something to be complained of. To the prince and the princess, the "gravity" is different at different times. Being a text or language, knowledge as well as the world has variety and change that can be associated with different positions.

Conclusion

I have thus argued for what I take to be fundamental differences of the two texts. However, I am not stating that they are completely different. It would be impossible to make a comparison in the first place if they had nothing at all to do with each other. In other words, the very act of comparison, if only in order to highlight differences, presumes a common ground which requires the recognition of similarities. I have worked on the assumption that both texts are linguistic constructs which produce as well as are produced by my reading or interpretation. Although they may present different views of the relationship between the world and language, they still do it in a similar way in language. One common point in relation to the idea of knowledge in both texts is that the narration has the authority and knows best anyway, because it is what the texts are made of. Such statements as "I will not attempt to describe what they had to go through for some time" ("Little Daylight" 152) and "Now the fact was that the old princess was at the root of the mischief" ("The Light Princess" 40) display the narrator as the one who knows the "fact" and who can decide what to tell and what not to tell. Even an apparent denial of knowledge is part of the narrative, as the sentence like "The exact preposition expressing this relation I do not happen to know" ("The Light Princess" 25) means that the preposition is something the narrator claims not to know. The narrator, by denouncing the knowledge, is therefore providing knowledge.

My own view of knowledge is similar to the one presented in "The Light Princess", and this is why I have referred to the details of the two texts. Language is not entirely transparent, nor is it entirely meaningless and arbitrary; in order to read, one has to pay attention to how language works. I admit that my interpretation of the two texts would not be universal, complete, or absolute;

after all, one cannot deal with all aspects of the text, if such a position exists. The reading I have given raises some theoretical questions concerning the way we read texts. That is to say, it suggests that there may be some things that are lost in the process of reading which assumes and focuses on similarities between texts. My reading of differences problematises the way a group of texts are treated as presenting a unified idea simply because they are supposed to be written by the same author. Within the field of MacDonald studies, this complicates critical narratives about "MacDonald" and his works; in a broader context, it also proposes to admit inconsistencies and contradictions in an author's oeuvre, inquiring at the same time what is involved in the notion of the "author" as subject. Moreover, my analysis of the two texts helps to show the problems that reside in generic readings, especially of what are generally classified as fairy tales. Genre classifications rely on the recognition of certain common features among texts, and this tends to predetermine and restrict the points of analysis. Readings of "fairy tales" frequently refer to the tales' "motifs" and "traditions", the definitions of which are often vague and which in any case have to do with limited aspects of the text, ignoring other elements. My suggestion is that texts need not always be read or discussed as fairy tales that are bound to a certain tale-type or structure, or as belonging to any particular genre or author for that matter; instead we may look at their details, which can lead to considerations of interesting ideas and problems.

Note

This is a revised and expanded version of the paper I presented at the 'George MacDonald Centenary Conference', University of Worcester, 2005. I would like to thank Dr Sue Walsh for reading the draft and giving me helpful advice.

Works Cited

Knoepflmacher, U. C., ed. *The Complete Fairy Tales*. By George MacDonald. New York: Penguin, 1999.
MacDonald, George. "The Light Princess". Knoepflmacher 15-53.
—. "Little Daylight". Knoepflmacher 149-64.
McGillis, Roderick, ed. *The Princess and the Goblin and The Princess and Curdie*. By George MacDonald. World's Classics. Oxford: Oxford University Press, 1990.
Raeper, William. *George MacDonald*. Tring: Lion, 1987.
Zipes, Jack. *Fairy Tales and the Art of Subversion: The Classical Genre for Children and the Process of Civilization*. 1983. New York: Routledge, 1988.

Chapter Five

"Natural History—The Heavenly Sort": George MacDonald's Integration of Faith and Reason

Larry E. Fink

Greville MacDonald recalled visiting his family the summer before Maurice, his brother, died:

> The summer of 1878 I was enabled to rejoin my people at Porto Fino. I had never seen my father in such good health: the great heat was a tonic to him. . . . We spent much of every day in the sea, so delightful was the little bay for swimming across to the peninsula standing across it. We had our own boat, and our father would take an oar upon occasion and pull with his boys . . . . Not the least my own pleasures was a new intimacy with my fourteen-year-old brother, Maurice, whom I was never to see again. We would have long talks about chemistry, physics and evolution, and I wondered at his instant and imaginative understanding"
> (*George MacDonald and His Wife* 488).

It is certain that the tone of those long talks would better be described as curious, open, and excited, as opposed to troubled and fretful, if, to even a small degree, the sons shared their father's attitude toward the sciences.

MacDonald's fearless search for truth—on both spiritual and physical levels—sets him apart from some of his contemporaries—and from some of ours. He felt free to question the Church, the Bible and Nature because of his undivided trust in the Christ of the gospels. In fact, he measured all else, including the New Testament epistles, against Christ, rather than reading the epistles as commentaries on the meaning of Christ's life. When he found the church of his experience inconsistent with the spirit of Christ, he veered from supposed orthodoxy. When the Bible appeared inconsistent or imperfect, he was not alarmed because his faith was in Christ, the living Word. And he revelled in the forms and phenomena of nature as the revelation of the intent and personality of Christ. In an 1884 letter to his sister-in-law, Charlotte Powell Godwin, he wrote:

> I believe in nothing else but Jesus Christ, in whom are all the mysteries of reality. Less than the story of him could not satisfy me, though less might give me hope. But if he be such as that story says, then all is well. If God be indeed such a God as satisfies Jesus, then hail to the world with all its summers and snows, all its delights and its aching, all its jubilance and its old age! We shall come out of it the sons and daughters of life, of God himself, the only Father. (Bordighera, last Sunday of 1884, The Beinecke)

Notice, MacDonald measures even the First Person of the Trinity against the Second, as revealed in the gospels.

Works from several genres-novels, fantasies, sermons and essays-reveal MacDonald's integration of faith and reason, religion and science. The title character of the somewhat autobiographical novel, *Robert Falconer* (1868), reflects MacDonald's allegiance to Christ above all: "He had ever one anchor of the soul, and he found that it held—the faith of Jesus (I say the faith of Jesus, not his own faith in Jesus), the truth of Jesus, the life of Jesus. . . . [I]n doing righteously, in loving mercy, in walking humbly, the conviction increased that Jesus knew the very secret of human life" (*Robert Falconer* 306). The passage alluded to, Micah 6.8, is one of the great touchstones of scripture, one especially suited to MacDonald's broad views: "He hath shewed thee, O man, what is good; and what doth the LORD require of thee, but to do justly, and to love mercy, and to walk humbly with thy God?" (KJV).

Robert also comments on time, process, and God's patience:

> Of one thing I am pretty sure, . . . that the same recipe Goethe gave for the enjoyment of life, applies equally to all work: "Do the thing that lies next you." That is all our business. Hurried results are worse than none. We must force nothing, but be partakers of the divine patience. How long it took to make the cradle! and we fret that the baby Humanity is not reading Euclid and Plato, even that it is not understanding the Gospel of St. John! If there is one thing evident in the world's history, it is that God hasteneth not. (353, 354)

One of his *Unspoken Sermons* (2nd Series) also reveals MacDonald's modern view of time and creation:

> Imagine, I say, the difficulty of such creation so great, that for it God must begin inconceivably far back in the infinitesimal regions of beginnings — not to say before anything in the least resembling man, but eternal miles beyond the last farthest-pushed discovery in protoplasm—to set in motion that division from himself which in its grand result should be individuality, consciousness, choice,

and conscious choice—choice at last pure, being the choice of the right, the true, the divinely harmonious. (qtd. in Raeper 247-248)

Returning to Robert Falconer, Robert comments on the sad condition of some women seen on the street: "They are in God's hands. . . . He hasn't done with them yet. Shall it take less time to make a woman than to make a world? Is not the woman the greater? She may have her ages of chaos, her centuries of crawling slime, yet rise a woman at last" (*Robert Falconer* 354). Again, Robert considers the time before humanity's emergence when he observes:

> Nothing excites me more . . . than a walk in the twilight through a crowded street . . . . because it is like the primordial chaos, a concentrated tumult of undetermined --possibilities. The germs of infinite adventure and result are floating around you like a snow-storm. You do not know what may arise in a moment and colour all your future. Out of this mass may suddenly start something marvellous, or, it may be, something you have been looking for for years. (*Robert Falconer* 349)

MacDonald was equally independent in his thinking about the Bible. Robert's mentor, Dr. Anderson speculates with Robert about the afterlife, saying, "I wadna like to tak to ony papistry; but I never cud mak oot frae the Bible . . . that it's a' ower wi' a body at their deith. I never heard them bring foret ony text but ane—the most ridiculous hash 'at ever ye heard—to justifee it" (321). Robert responds, "I ken the text ye mean—'As the tree falleth so it shall lie'...", (Ecclesiastes 11.3). He and the Doctor quickly dismiss the application of this passage as a valid argument against any hope of salvation after death. Dr. Anderson goes on to discuss his "old Brahmin friend" from his days in India:

> The first comman'ment was a' he kent. He loved God—nae a God like Jesus Christ, but the God he kent—and that was all he could. . . . Still there was religion in him; and he who died for the sins o' the whole world has surely been revealed to him lang er' noo, and throu the knowledge o' him, he noo dwalls in that God efter whom he aspired. (323)

MacDonald also paints a comical picture of a character he calls "a combative Bible-reader" (339). Robert overhears this "Bible thumper"-as they are called in Texas-berating the honest atheist, Mr. De Fleuri.

> [De Fleuri's] silence and apparent impassiveness angered the irreverent little worthy. To Falconer's humour he looked a vulgar bull-terrier barking at a noble, sad-faced staghound. His foolish arguments against infidelity, drawn from Paley's *Natural Theology*, and tracts about the inspiration of the Bible, touched

the sore-hearted unbelief of the man no nearer than the clangour of negro kettles affects the eclipse of the sun. (340)

Finally, Robert steps in and easily dismantles the evangelist's logic and sends him on his way. Then he says to the unbeliever, "Mr. De Fleuri, I believe in God with all my heart, and soul, and strength, and mind; though not in that poor creature's arguments. I don't know that your unbelief is not better than his faith" (340). (Tennyson comes to mind: "There lives more faith in honest doubt, / Believe me, than in half the creeds" [*In Memorium*, section 96]).

But perhaps it is in the Curdie books that MacDonald reveals his comfortable attitude toward the ideas of an old earth and creation by evolution. In *The Princess & the Goblin*, these ideas are embodied in the goblins themselves, devolved from humanity, over countless generations. The narrator explains the origin of the Goblins:

> There was a legend current in the country, that at one time they lived above ground, and were very like other people. But for some reason or other, concerning which there were different legendary theories. . . . they had all taken refuge in the subterranean caverns, whence they never came out but at night, and then seldom showed themselves in any numbers, and never to many people at once. . . . Those who caught sight of any of them said they had greatly altered in the course of generations; and no wonder, seeing they lived away from the sun, in cold and wet and dark places.
> (*The Princess & the Goblin* 6)

In *The Princess & Curdie*, however, MacDonald develops the idea more fully to support one of his central themes—that is, that God wants each person to change, to become the particular person that He had in mind in creating each.

The Princess and Curdie begins with a lyrical description of mountains and their origins, with the mention of "millions of ages—ever since the earth flew off from the sun, a great blot of fire, and began to cool" (3), certainly not a literal reading of Genesis. Repeatedly, MacDonald uses the word "change" to describe the emergence of a mountain. This is an ideal beginning for a novel that uses physical change as a metaphor for spiritual change. He speculates on the possibility of eyeless fish in lightless underground rivers and asks: ". . . who can tell?—and whoever can't tell is free to think--. . . " (*Curdie* 3). This freedom to think or imagine based on what one knows is an important element in MacDonald's approach to theological as well as scientific questions. In *Robert Falconer*, the narrator muses, "Some people take comfort from the true eyes of a dog—and a precious thing to the loving heart is the love of even a dumb animal" (216). His footnote to this sentence reads:

> Why should Sir Walter Scott, who felt the death of Camp, his bull terrier, so much that he declined a dinner engagement in consequence, say on the death of his next favorite, a greyhound . . . —"Rest her body, since I dare not say soul!'"? Where did he get that "dare not"? Is it well that the daring of genius should be circumscribed by an unbelief so common-place as to be capable only of subscription? (216)

Of course, this kind of free thinking is what lost MacDonald his pulpit at Arundel.

Another parallel between Curdie and Robert is worth mentioning. Of course, both characters grow from childhood to adulthood. (The three parts of *Robert Falconer* are titled "His Boyhood", "His Youth", and "His Manhood.") But both books also allude to or echo Coleridge's "Rhyme of the Ancient Mariner"—a tale of revelation and transformation. The allusions are explicit in *Robert Falconer*, less so in *The Princess and Curdie*. For instance, when the narrator asks why he was chosen to work with Robert, Robert replies with three lines from Coleridge:

> The moment that his face I see,
> I know the man that must hear me:
> To him my tale I teach. (*Robert Falconer* 363)

And in another passage, we read, "'Na, na,' whispered the manufacturer, laying, like the Ancient Mariner, a brown skinny hand of restraint upon Robert's arm—'na, na, never heed her'" (*Robert Falconer* 264). Curdie's transformation, like the Mariner's, begins with the same act of thoughtless violence: he shoots a bird with his bow and arrow. The Mariner never says why he shot the Albatross with his crossbow, but by the close of the poem it is clear that he simply did not recognize it as a beautiful and living creature, thus worthy of his love. Curdie is in exactly the same situation, as MacDonald explains: ". . . not until this very moment had he ever known what a pigeon was" (*Curdie* 15). Curdie had become more and more like his fellow miners; ". . . he was getting rather stupid—one of the chief signs of which was that he believed less and less in things he had never seen" (12). "He was gradually changing into a commonplace man" (12). By the time Curdie shoots the pigeon, "He was not the Curdie he had been meant to be" (15). He learns from this experience and from Irene's great-great grandmother, that in not trying to become better, he was becoming worse. He admits to her, "I was doing the wrong of never wanting or trying to be better" (27). She responds, "You have got it, Curdie. . . . When people don't care to be better they must be doing everything wrong" (27). She urges him, "Do better, and grow better, and be better" (28). So, change, for better or worse, is inevitable—a favourite theme of MacDonald's beloved Romantics. In his view, one must choose to become better, or he will become worse.

At this point, the divine figure, the grandmother, gives Curdie a gift that will help him accomplish the mission she is sending him on. She asks him if he has "ever heard what some philosophers say—that men were all animals once?" "No, ma'am", he answers. She responds, "It is of no consequence. But there is another thing that is of the greatest consequence—this: that all men, if they do not take care, go down the hill to the animal's country; that many men are actually, all their lives, going to be beasts" (71-72). She describes his gift: ". . . you will henceforth be able to know at once the hand of a man who is growing into a beast; nay more—you will at once feel the foot of the beast that he is growing [into]. . ." (73). Curdie is also given a travelling companion—a grotesquely ugly dog-like animal with large teeth and powerful jaws. When he is introduced to her, the grandmother says, "Give Curdie a paw, Lina." Taking her paw with a shudder of "terrified delight" he felt "the soft, neat little hand of a child" (76). Later, Curdie explains, "I believe . . . that Lina is a woman, and that she was naughty, but is now growing good" (160). In that first meeting with Lina, the grandmother tells Curdie, "That paw in your hand now might almost teach you the whole science of natural history—the heavenly sort, I mean" (77).

As interested as MacDonald was in the natural history of the earth and its creatures, he was more interested in this "heavenly sort" of natural history—that is, the process by which he could become the self God intended him to become by exercising his will to do the next good thing at hand. In both realms, change is built in; it is inevitable. Transformation appears to be inseparable from the Creator's art. And MacDonald seems to have welcomed this scheme and all its potential for spiritual allegorizing.

One hundred years after MacDonald's death-146 years after the publication of *The Origin of Species*-questions about the age of the earth and human origins still trouble many people—particularly in the United States. These issues divide believers and distract them from more important issues and missions. MacDonald's informed, imaginative integration of faith and reason offers a model for others on a quest for wholeness. It is clear that an active and receptive imagination is essential in this process of integration. C. S. Lewis wrote *The Abolition of Man* in response to educators who believed:

> . . . that the best thing they can do is to fortify the minds of young people against emotion. My own experience as a teacher tells an opposite tale. For every one pupil who needs to be guarded from a weak excess of sensibility there are

three who need to be awakened from the slumber of cold vulgarity. (*Abolition of Man* 13)

He concluded that ". . . a good education should build some sentiments while destroying others" (14). MacDonald might add that a good education should nurture and expand the imagination, not foster either-or thinking, literalism, and its offspring, legalism. In his 1880 essay, "A Sketch of Individual Development", he outlines in detail the multi-step process by which the imagination and the reason—personified as Lady Poetry and Madame Science—can be reconciled in the adult mind:

> . . . at the entrance of Science, nobly and gracefully as she bears herself, young Poetry shrinks back startled, dismayed. Poetry is as true as Science, and Science is holy as Poetry; but young Poetry is timid and Science is fearless, and bears with her a colder atmosphere than the other has learned to brave. It is not that Madame Science shows any antagonism to Lady Poetry; but the atmosphere and plane on which alone they can meet as friends who understand each other, is the mind and heart of the sage, not the boy.
> ('Individual Development' 51)

In the first century, St. Paul addressed a divisive issue in his letter to the Romans; the question was whether it was right for believers to eat food of a certain kind. Paul gave specific advice about lovingly making allowances for others' opinions and sensibilities and concluded with one of those touchstone passages—like Micah 6.8, cited above—that MacDonald surely loved: ". . . the kingdom of God is not meat and drink; but righteousness, and peace, and joy in the Holy Ghost" (Romans 14.17 KJV). Nor is the kingdom of God when and how God created the world and its inhabitants. We can be grateful that one hundred years after his death, MacDonald's fiction—and non fiction—still have the power to awaken the imagination from the "slumber of cold vulgarity" and lead the reader toward a mature integration of faith and reason.

The practical implications for education that follow would include two positive actions and one important omission. Education should include 1) the thorough nourishing of the student's imagination and 2) a compelling introduction to brave Madame Science in all her elegant complexity. Absent should be the strident, matter-of-fact voices of adults--believers and unbelievers--whose imaginations are too cramped to allow room for integration to occur in their own minds. Then, perhaps, might more students develop the mind of the sage, where poetry and science can meet as friends.

Works Cited

Lewis, C. S. *The Abolition of Man* (1944). San Francisco: Harper Collins, 2001.

MacDonald, George. "A Sketch of Individual Development." *A Dish of Orts: Chiefly Papers on the Imagination and on Shakespeare* (1908). Norwood Editions, 1977, 43-76.

—. *Letter to Charlotte Powell Godwin*, December, 1884, The Beinecke Rare Book and Manuscript Library, Yale U.

—. *The Princess and Curdie* (1882). London: Puffin Books, 1994.

—. *The Princess and the Goblin* (1872). Oxford: Oxford University Press, 1990.

—. *Robert Falconer* (1868). Whitethorn, California: Johannesen, 1995.

MacDonald, Greville. *George MacDonald and His Wife* (1824). Whitethorn, California: Johannesen, 1998.

Raeper, William. *George MacDonald*. Tring: Lion Publishing, 1987.

CHAPTER SIX

MACDONALD AND PULLMAN, OR: (GREAT-GREAT-) GRANDFATHER GEORGE

WILLIAM GRAY

> "Just as we can never embrace ... a single person, but embrace the whole of her or his family romance, so we can never read a poet without reading the whole of his or her family romance as a poet."
> (Harold Bloom, *The Anxiety of Influence* 94)

Introduction

This essay is an attempt to explore some possible relationships between the fantasy writing of George MacDonald and that of Philip Pullman. Such an attempt needs, however, to take account of Harold Bloom's warning against the error of treating poets as if they were self-contained individuals. In *The Anxiety of Influence* Bloom is admittedly making specific reference to the relations between lyric poets, whereas the work to be discussed in the present essay is fantasy writing in prose. Nevertheless I believe that Bloom's analysis of the "family romances" of "poets as poets" can be adapted to apply to writers in other literary genres, and to the so-to-speak "familial" relations that constitute a writer as a creative literary individual. Indeed, Bloom himself sought in his 1980 paper "*Clinamen*: Towards a Theory of Fantasy" to apply his "anxiety of influence" theory not only to the genealogy of the literary *genre* - or rather sub-genre (Bloom, *Clinamen* 2) - of fantasy, but also to the relationships between particular pieces of fantasy writing, for example the relation of his own *The Flight to Lucifer* to David Lindsay's *A Voyage to Arcturus*. Of course the gender bias of Bloom's famous theory of "the anxiety of influence" was long ago pointed out by Sandra Gilbert and Susan Gubar in their *The Madwoman in the Attic*; this is an issue to which I shall return later in this essay. What I hope to show in this essay is that however tenuous and complex the "family" connections that link Pullman and MacDonald may be, they tend to be dominated by another figure who is closely and inextricably associated with both of them: C.S. Lewis. Lewis figures, firstly, as a bad father to Pullman, an inevitable precursor whose writing seems to fascinate as well as repel Pullman. Secondly, Lewis appears as MacDonald's dutiful son, devoted to his spiritual (if not literary) master. Ultimately, however, there seems to me to be something hollow and unconvincing about both these versions of a filial relationship. In the first place, Lewis is arguably not the moral monster that Pullman makes him out to be; and secondly, MacDonald is more than just the spiritual director (important as that is) that Pullman presents us with. For one thing, MacDonald is, I will argue, a much better writer than Lewis would have us believe. Pullman and Lewis could thus be seen as "framing" their precursors, in all the senses of Barbara Johnson's memorable usage of the term "frame"[viii]. However, it is Harold Bloom's "map of misreading", in its own way as arcane as Johnson's poststructuralist subtleties, that seems more apt here, and more in tune with the Gnostic sympathies of both Pullman and MacDonald.

Without venturing too far into the battery of explicitly Gnostic categories that Bloom elaborates in *The Anxiety of Influence* and *A Map of Misreading*, one might suggest that it is the first two of his six strategies for misreading–or "revisionary ratios", as Bloom calls them – that might seem to apply most readily to the relationships that are the subject of the present paper. *Clinamen* (or "swerving'") might arguably apply to the relation of Philip Pullman and C.S. Lewis, with the former "swerving" away from his precursor in a corrective movement. Bloom's second "revisionary ratio" *tessera* (or "antithetical completion") might seem more appropriate to the way in which C.S. Lewis (as we hope to show below) "antithetically completes his precursor, by so reading [MacDonald's work] as to retain its terms but to mean them in another sense, as though the precursor had failed to go far enough" (Bloom, *Anxiety* 14). However, Bloom's six "revisionary ratios" are so general - Bloom himself is quite undogmatic about their number, their names and their application – that it is difficult to be very precise in applying them. In the context of the present discussion, I propose simply to use Bloom's general idea that a writer must necessarily *misread* a significant precursor in order to achieve his own identity as a writer. Gilbert and Gubar have argued (referring *en passant* to MacDonald's *Lilith*) that *The Anxiety of Influence* depends on a patriarchal Oedipal scenario (Gilbert and Gubar 46-51). While I intend to argue that there is a degree of Bloomian misreading involved both in the relationship of Pullman to C.S. Lewis, and of Lewis to George MacDonald, I also intend ultimately to retain a degree of suspicion towards the Oedipal focus of Bloom's approach.

Pullman explicitly gives his own version of his literary origins in the "Acknowledgements" that conclude the "His Dark Materials" trilogy. He writes: "I have stolen ideas from every book I have ever read. My principle in researching for a novel is 'Read like a butterfly, write like a bee', and if this story contains any honey, it is entirely because of the quality of the nectar I found in the work of better writers" (Pullman *Amber Spyglass* 549). While this description smacks rather more of free love than of the obsessive Oedipal conflicts of the Bloomian nuclear family, there is nevertheless an interestingly masculinist subtext to its intertext. The phrase "Float like a butterfly, sting like a bee" originated of course with Cassius Clay (later "Muhammed Ali"), than whom a stronger expression of male self-creation through conflict would be hard to find - with Sonny Liston perhaps figuring as the Bad Daddy in this Oedipal psychodrama. The suggestion that Pullman is, like Ali, "the Greatest" is reinforced by the quotations on the covers of Pullman's books: "Is [Philip Pullman] the best storyteller ever?" and "Move over Tolkien and C.S. Lewis...". Admittedly this "hype" does not necessarily reflect Pullman's own views, though the extraordinarily ambitious scope of 'His Dark Materials' has not escaped some critical suspicions of hubris.[ix] Pullman is by any standards a "strong" poet or writer, and one unafraid of flaunting his literary lineage. Though Pullman himself has been in some respects critical of postmodernism[x], some critics have found in his work an (inter)textually promiscuous postmodern pluralism. Such postmodern intertextual promiscuity notwithstanding, there is nevertheless one figure with whom it seems Pullman must contend above all others, and that is C.S. Lewis. This encounter seems susceptible of a Bloomian interpretation as an Oedipal misreading of a literary father-figure.

Philip Pullman and C.S. Lewis

Pullman has frequently and publicly attacked Lewis, most notoriously perhaps in his article "The Dark Side of Narnia" which vilifies the "pernicious" Narnia series as "one of the most ugly and poisonous things I've ever read" on account of "the misogyny, the racism, the sado-masochistic relish for violence that permeates it"[xi]. While none of these charges against Lewis is new, nor perhaps entirely unfounded, it is in fact the "relish for violence that permeates" Pullman's attack on Lewis that is most striking. Lewis seems too close to Pullman for the latter's comfort. Pullman clearly feels the need to distinguish his own work from what seems to the innocent eye to be the rather similar work of Lewis. Specific textual correspondences could be multiplied: for example, in the first book of both the 'His Dark Materials' trilogy and the *The Chronicles of Narnia* the heroine (even the names "Lyra" and "Lucy" are not dissimilar - Blake's "Lyca"[xii] notwithstanding) makes a momentous discovery in a wardrobe. However, it is the general thematic similarities that are most striking: both Pullman and Lewis have written fantasy with a religious (or quasi-religious) angle about growing up, with lots of intertextual allusions. If Pullman in an interview has called the "His Dark Materials" trilogy "*Paradise Lost* for teenagers in three volumes"[xiii], then Lewis's *The Silver Chair* has been called "the *Faerie Queen* in miniature" (Myers 157). Of course, according to Pullman, his fantasy is not really fantasy, though his claim in the same interview that *Northern Lights* is "not fantasy ...[but] a work of stark realism" (Squires 17) seems to be somewhat tenuously based on his alleged superiority over the likes of Tolkien in the portrayal of psychology. Pullman is apparently anti-religious, though Hugh Rayment-Pickard in *The Devil's Account: Philip Pullman and Christianity* does not have to work very hard to disengage Pullman's 'hidden theology'. Rayment-Pickard forbears from any accusation of disingenuousness on Pullman's part, suggesting only that the latter's claim not to have a "message", being merely a story-teller, is a kind of blind spot (Rayment-Pickard 23). Pullman clearly does have a "message" that is in certain crucial respects different from Lewis's Christian one; however, the practical moral outcomes seem *mutatis mutandis* pretty similar, as is evident in the following passage from *The Amber Spyglass* where the angel Xaphania offers Will and Lyra these words of wisdom:

> And if you help everyone else in your worlds to do that, by helping them to learn and understand about themselves and each other and the way everything works, and by showing how to be kind instead of cruel, and patient instead of hasty, and cheerful instead of surly, and above all how to keep their minds open and free and curious ... (Pullman, *Amber Spyglass* 520)

Evidently Lewis has no monopoly on preaching, for Pullman shows himself here to be just as capable of didacticism as the next children's author.

The real sites of conflict between Pullman and Lewis in this Oedipal struggle are, unsurprisingly, sex and death. Pullman specifically takes issue with two scenes in Lewis's *The Last Battle*. Firstly, he criticises Lewis for excluding Susan from "the real Narnia", or Heaven, on account of her being "interested in nothing nowadays except nylons and lipstick and invitations" (Lewis, *Last Battle* 124). This passage is often seen as some kind of sexist and/or puritan and/or misogynist attack on female sexuality, for which the nylons and lipstick and invitations are metonyms. Pullman accuses Lewis of a kind of prudish condemnation of adolescent sexuality, which he by contrast seeks to celebrate in the scene at the end of *The Amber Spyglass* where Will and Lyra mutually stroke their demons' fur, an activity that presumably refers metonymically to some kind of sexual intimacy. However, Lewis has arguably been rather harshly treated on this issue. The problem with Susan is not so much her adolescent sexuality as such, but rather the fact that she allows the *construction* of that sexuality to be so all-absorbing that she doesn't *want* anything else. And you don't have to be sexist and/or puritan and/or misogynist to worry about what our culture does to teenage girls. When Lyra and Will begin to explore their sexuality, they are still involved in a heroic quest; that's precisely what Susan – sadly - doesn't seem to want anymore.

Secondly. Pullman criticises Lewis for his allegedly "horrible" message that being killed in a train crash is the best thing ever if you end up in Heaven[xiv]. Apart from the fact that "His Dark Materials" is at least as violent as anything that Lewis ever wrote, Lewis's Platonism by no means necessarily implies a devaluation, let alone a hatred, of this world, but only some care in our dealings with it. There is always a danger of conflating Platonism and Manichaeism. The latter *is* precisely world-hating, since for it Creation is actually the Fall, and consequently the world and the flesh are merely snares (or indeed "tombs") from which the Manichaean adept seeks only escape – though sometimes not just yet, as one famous ex-Manichaean once pleaded (Augustine, *Confessions* 8:7)! That famous ex-Manichaean, Augustine of Hippo, was acutely aware of the importance of discriminating between on the one hand Manichaeism, which despite the claims of its adherents was profoundly anti-Christian, and on the other hand Platonism, which was in Augustine's mature view compatible with Christian faith, though of course insufficient on its own[xv]. C.S. Lewis stands in a long line of Christian Platonists for whom the world and the body are, as the good creations of a good God, capable of expressing divine beauty and wisdom. That human beings are perennially prone to idolize, degrade and exploit that which if used properly should reflect the glory of God, is the problem of sin or evil. The point is that Christian Platonism, far from being world-hating, wants the world and the body to be used in the right way, that is, as images of the divine life. In this sense it is deeply world-affirming. The difficulty is that Platonism, like Christian faith itself, is dialectical, since the very desire that leads ultimately to God is dangerously powerful and always prone to short-circuiting the spiritual (and not only the spiritual) system by seeking premature fulfilment or joy. And joy prematurely grasped inevitably turns out to be mere pleasure or "thrills". All of this is made abundantly clear in Lewis's deeply Augustinian spiritual autobiography, *Surprised by Joy*.[xvi]

Pullman, then, is perfectly entitled to proclaim some kind of this-worldly message; however, firstly, it is not the case that in order to do so he has necessarily to misread Lewis as a quasi-Manichaean (though a Bloomian reading might claim precisely that he *does* have to); and secondly, Pullman's purported this-worldliness appears less than consistent. It seems rather odd, for example, that a self-proclaimed this-worldly atheist should allow any sort of post-mortem existence whatsoever, as in the world of the dead sequence in *The Amber Spyglass* when, in a kind of reversal of the Orpheus and Eurydice myth, Lyra goes to find and rescue her friend Roger who has been captured and killed by "the Gobblers". More significantly, the ghosts escaping from the world of the dead are seen to achieve a kind of blissful release in a moment of mystic pantheism that is again rather hard to reconcile with a rigorous this-worldly atheism. As Lyra reassures the ghosts, reading the alethiometer:

> But your daemons en't just *nothing* now; they're part of everything. All the atoms that were them, they've gone into the air and the wind and the trees and the earth and all the living things. They'll never vanish. They're just part of everything. And that's exactly what'll happen to you ... (*Amber Spyglass* 335)

One of the ghosts takes up Lyra's theme: "[W]e'll be alive again in a thousand blades of grass, and a million leaves, we'll be falling in the raindrops and blowing in the fresh breeze, we'll be glittering in the dew under the stars and the moon ..." (*Amber Spyglass* 336). And when the ghost of Lyra's old friend Roger becomes the first to achieve release from the world of the dead, it is presented as a moment of intoxication: "He took a step forward, and turned to look back at Lyra, and laughed in surprise as he found himself turning into the night, the starlight, the air ... and then he was gone, leaving behind such a vivid little burst of happiness that Will was reminded of the bubbles in a glass of champagne" (*Amber Spyglass* 382). Pullman at this point seems very close, *mutatis mutandis*, to the Romantic pantheism of Wordsworth, as expressed for example in "A slumber did my spirit seal"-though with an ambivalence and ambiguity admittedly foreign to Pullman's "Happy Hour" version of pantheistic mystical surrender:

> No motion has she now, no force;
>   She neither hears nor sees;
> Rolled round in earth's diurnal course,
>   With rocks, and stones, and trees.
> William Wordsworth "A slumber did my spirit seal" 1799

There is even a hint in Pullman's text at this point of something not dissimilar to MacDonald's notion of the "good death'" which the young Lewis picked up on (Lewis, *MacDonald Anthology* 21). The "good death" motif is in part a version of the Romantic principle of "stirb und werde" [die and become]; it is perhaps most strangely expressed in the aëranth or flying fish which dives into the boiling pot in *The Golden Key*–the latter is incidentally the only MacDonald text that Pullman says he actually remembers reading[xvii]. Perhaps there lies, behind Pullman's inconsistent (but in a Bloomian sense necessary) misreading of Lewis, a family resemblance to the literary father figure that Lewis in his turn misread, George MacDonald.

C.S. Lewis and George MacDonald

If Pullman's misreading of Lewis is an act of vilification, Lewis's misreading of MacDonald is an act of sanctification. Lewis claimed MacDonald as his spiritual master, and famously said: "I fancy I have never written a book in which I did not quote from him" (Lewis, *MacDonald Anthology* 20). For Lewis, MacDonald was "the greatest genius" as a maker of myths, of "fantasy that hovers between the allegorical and the mythopoeic" (Lewis, *MacDonald Anthology* 16; 14). However, Lewis did not rate MacDonald as a writer; in literary terms MacDonald was, according to Lewis, not even second-rate:

> In making these extracts I have been concerned with MacDonald not as a writer but as a Christian teacher. If I were to deal with him as a writer, as a man of letters, I would be faced with a difficult critical problem. If we define Literature as an art whose medium is words, then certainly MacDonald has no place in its first rank– perhaps not even in its second. There are indeed passages…where the wisdom and (I would dare to call it) the holiness that are in him triumph over and even burn away the baser elements in his style: the expression becomes precise, weighty, economic; acquires a cutting edge. But he does not maintain this level for long. The texture of his writing as a whole is undistinguished, at times fumbling. (Lewis, *MacDonald Anthology* 14)[xviii]

It is noteworthy that even those elements of MacDonald's style that satisfy Lewis's perhaps over-sensitive critical palate are attributed to the holiness of MacDonald the Christian teacher, rather than to the skill of MacDonald the professional writer. Lewis's assertion that " the texture of [MacDonald's] writing *as a whole* is undistinguished" (Lewis, *MacDonald Anthology* 14, emphasis added) seems to disallow the move which would interpret his criticisms of MacDonald's writing style as applying only to the "realist" novels, but not to the fantasy works. Lewis does make a sharp qualitative distinction between the two bodies of MacDonald's work: "[MacDonald's] great works are *Phantastes,* the *Curdie* books, *The Golden Key, The Wise Woman,* and *Lilith*…. they are supremely good in their own kind … The meaning, the suggestion, the radiance, is incarnate in the whole story …" (Lewis, *MacDonald Anthology* 17). But the transcendent supremacy of this "canon within the canon" of MacDonald's oeuvre is not made on the basis of any literary merit, since Lewis has already precluded any serious consideration of MacDonald as a literary artist. According to Lewis, MacDonald's artistic achievement is not a literary one at all, but rather belongs to what Lewis calls mythopoeic fantasy. Lewis hesitates to discuss the latter in strictly literary terms since, as myth, it is for Lewis in principle independent of language: "Myth does not essentially exist in *words* at all. We all agree that the story of Balder is a great myth, a thing of inexhaustible value. But whose version – whose *words* – are we thinking when we say this?" (Lewis, *MacDonald Anthology* 15) As evidence of this claim, Lewis offers the anecdote of his hearing the story of Kafka's *The Castle* related in conversation and afterwards reading the book for himself. He claims, incredibly enough for those attuned to the disturbing quality of Kafka's prose, that "the reading added nothing." (Lewis, *MacDonald Anthology* 16) The date of publication of Lewis's *MacDonald Anthology* (1946) suggests that here Lewis was not consciously going against the Spirit of the Age and the mid-twentieth century "linguistic turn", although he was quite capable of (and indeed, one suspects, would have relished) such deliberate provocation[xix]. Lewis's view that Myth has a power and value 'independent of its embodiment in any literary work' (Lewis, *Experiment* 41) may have a certain immediate plausibility, but it runs counter to the prevailing intellectual climate of the latter half of the twentieth century, which might be summed up in the slogan deriving from Derrida's *On Grammatology: "Il n'y a pas de hors-texte"* ("there is nothing outside of the text") (Norton 1825). More concretely, current debates about the success (or otherwise) of the translation of *The Lord of the Rings,* and indeed *The Lion, the Witch and the Wardrobe,* into film versions would seem to raise questions about Lewis's assertion of the myth's in-principle independence of its literary form. It is also noteworthy how critics in areas other than literature (Lewis's examples are mime and film) tend to describe their particular medium in quasi-linguistic terms.[xx] I suspect I am not alone in finding it hard to accept Lewis's claim that "the meaning, the suggestion, the radiance" that is "incarnate" in MacDonald's great works (Lewis, *MacDonald Anthology* 17) is merely "a particular pattern of events which would equally delight and nourish if it had reached me by some medium which involved no words at all" (Lewis, *MacDonald Anthology* 15)[xxi]. Indeed, in his edition of MacDonald's *Complete Fairy Tales,* U.C. Knoepflmacher has specifically blamed Lewis's influence (particularly through the latter's *MacDonald Anthology*) for the lack of critical attention to what he calls "the rhetorical sophistication of [MacDonald's] best work", so that:

> MacDonald's profoundly experimental and inter-textual fairy tales and fantasies, his subversive incursions into so many different nineteenth-century literary forms, and his delight in the friction and contradictions he could produce through his generic criss-crossings, went unnoted (Knoepflmacher viii-ix).

One example of MacDonald's stylistic virtuosity might be the fourth sentence of "The Wise Woman" which takes over 400 words to lead up to the bare fact that "something happened" (Knoepflmacher 225-6). This might even be seen as a kind of prescient ironic commentary on Lewis's claim that what matters is the "events" which need no words at all, so that "[i]f the story is anywhere embodied in words, that is almost an accident" (Lewis, *MacDonald Anthology* 15). Lewis's doubtful theory of language thus allows him to celebrate MacDonald's acts of myth-making genius, despite the latter's alleged shortcomings as a writer. Whether Pullman would welcome being placed alongside MacDonald as a creator of myths is uncertain. I suspect, though, that Pullman, who evidently takes considerable pains over his literary style, would hardly relish being damned with Lewis's faint praise when the latter separates the power of a myth from its actual literary expression. Such damnation with faint praise is precisely one of the ways in which Lewis arguably "misreads" MacDonald. Whatever reservations one might have about MacDonald's "realist" fiction, for the most part his fantasy fiction is brilliantly written. And this is not simply a case of style (or indeed formal experimentation) for its own sake. The *content* of, for example, *The Light Princess*-which interestingly is not listed in Lewis's "canon within the [MacDonald] canon"-is literally inseparable from its literary *form*. In the meaning of this tale, the tone of its narration is crucial: levity is what it is all about.

However, Lewis not only attacks MacDonald's potency as a writer, whilst all the while praising him as a spiritual master who through his mythopoeic genius baptised Lewis's imagination (Lewis, *MacDonald Anthology* 21; *Surprised by Joy* 146); he also misreads the theological *content* of MacDonald's work. This is particularly relevant to a comparison of Pullman and MacDonald since the theology of C.S. Lewis to which Pullman objects is not necessarily to be identified with MacDonald's, despite the fact that Lewis has co-opted the latter. In her paper "George MacDonald and C.S. Lewis" in William Raeper's *The Gold Thread,* Catherine Durie shows how Lewis systematically misread MacDonald's theology. One important aspect of MacDonald's theology that Lewis "quietly drops" is what Durie calls "the childlikeness of God", and its corollary that: "MacDonald consistently claims that theology misrepresents God when it portrays him as the great king"(Raeper, *Gold Thread* 173). MacDonald's view of God is, says Durie, "a long way from the hierarchical and authoritative images that move Lewis" (Raeper, *Gold Thread* 173). Lewis's misreadings of MacDonald culminate in *The Great Divorce* when he makes the *character* "George MacDonald" express views directly opposite to views the real MacDonald actually held. As Durie puts it:

> Lewis and MacDonald are here made to change places; but the MacDonald who makes such forceful points is a ventriloquist's dummy. It is Lewis's voice which subverts the real MacDonald's belief in hell as a temporary purifying force, and heaven as the home of every one of God's children. (Raeper, *Gold Thread* 175)

These misreadings of MacDonald by Lewis bear directly on issues that Pullman has raised in relation to Lewis. Firstly, Pullman's idea of "the republic of heaven" depends precisely on his opposition to the idea of God as king (an opposition which MacDonald shared, but Lewis edited out). Secondly, on the issue of universal salvation, Lewis actively misrepresents MacDonald and makes him reject the idea of universalism that MacDonald actually espoused, and according to which not only the mildly rebellious Susan, but also the seriously rebellious Satan (or "Samoil", as he appears in *Lilith*[xxii]), will ultimately be saved (MacDonald, *Lilith* 217-8). So even if Lewis does let Susan be damned (in both senses of "let"), then MacDonald certainly wouldn't. This raises the possibility that Pullman may have more in common with MacDonald than we would expect if we assumed that MacDonald and Lewis shared identical (and to Pullman offensive) theological views.

MacDonald and Pullman

What then could MacDonald and Pullman be seen to have in common? First of all, a faith in stories, and more specifically, stories that appeal to what MacDonald called "the fantastic imagination" (I put it this way partly to circumvent Pullman's avowed dislike of the genre "fantasy literature"). Stories, and more specifically fairy stories, are a way of communicating in a non-conceptual way; for MacDonald it is a kind of category mistake to expect a fairy tale "to impart anything defined, anything notionally recognizable" (Knoepflmacher 8). MacDonald's view of language not only echoes (especially German) Romanticism; it also seems to prefigure Kristeva's distinction between "the Symbolic" and "the Semiotic" (or "phenotext" and the "genotext") (Norton 2169-79)[xxiii] when he replies to the claim that words–unlike music–"are meant and fitted to carry a precise meaning":

> It is very seldom indeed that they carry the exact meaning of any user of them! And if they can be so used as to convey definite meaning, it does not follow that they ought never to carry anything else. ... They can convey a scientific fact, or throw a shadow of her child's dream on the heart of a mother. (Knoepflmacher 8)

This idea that "Sometimes fairy stories may best say what's to be said" is of course particularly associated with Lewis (see Lewis, *On This and Other Worlds*), but he certainly didn't invent it; it was the common property of other Inklings such as Tolkien and Barfield and derives ultimately from Romanticism and especially perhaps German Romanticism. Lewis's version of the concrete imaginative experience of myth versus the abstract intellectual understanding of allegory tends to be set up in a way that resonates with the New Critical privileging of the organic unity of a non-conceptual, non- paraphrasable transcendental meaning (see Gray, *Lewis* 33). This derives principally from Coleridge, with the emphasis on the organic unity of meaning; but there is also a different kind of Romanticism which stresses, if not the indeterminacy of meaning, then at least the diversity of meaning as received differently by different hearers. I use 'hearers' advisedly because in MacDonald's essay 'The Fantastic Imagination' the key example for how art communicates is music or the sonata (Knoepflmacher 8-9). As MacDonald puts it: "The greatest forces lie in the region of the uncomprehended" (Knoepflmacher 9).

The positing of music as the condition to which all the arts aspire was central to German Romanticism (whence the later European Symbolist movement took the idea[xxiv]). Pullman too has related his writing to musical experience. In the powerful final sequence of *Northern Lights/Golden Compass*, when Lyra (and indeed the reader) is moving into "the region of the uncomprehended" as she advances into another world, Lord Asriel cries: "Can you feel that wind? A wind from another world!" (*Northern Lights/Golden Compass* 394). This explicitly echoes the line "Ich fühle luft von anderen planeten" ("I feel air from other planets") from the poem "Entrückung" by the German Symbolist poet Stefan George. Pullman has intertextually related the effect of this transition into another world to Schoenberg's setting of George's poem in his String Quartet No. 2, when the music leaves the world of tonality altogether and moves into the strange new world of atonality[xxv]. Here, in an archetypally Romantic gesture, literary Symbolism (George's poem) fuses with music (Schoenberg's Quartet) and illuminates the strange power of this numinous moment in Pullman's novel which stretches towards a kind of *mysterium tremendum et fascinans*, as Rudolf Otto famously described the experience "The Holy". Lyra's first full experience of the Aurora or "Northern Lights" had moved her to tears with a vision which "was so beautiful it was almost holy" (*Northern Lights/Golden Compass* 183), though perhaps we might have expected the rhetoric of "the sublime" rather than 'the beautiful" for a sight whose "immensity ... was scarcely conceivable" (*Northern Lights/Golden Compass* 183). The Romantic register returns at the climax of the novel when the Aurora is described, for example, as "a cataract of glory" (*Northern Lights/Golden Compass* 392). This rhetoric of the sublime and the numinous seems to echo the claim of MacDonald - whose supreme gift according to Lewis was to mediate "Holiness" (Lewis, *Surprised by Joy* 145) - that it was supremely in music and (in the widest sense) the fairy tale, those products of "the fantastic imagination", that we encounter those "greatest forces [that] lie in the region of the uncomprehended" (Knoepflmacher 9).

Such attunement to the diverse possibilities of interpretation - Lyra relates her numinous experience of the Aurora to her trance-like state while consulting the alethiometer (*Northern Lights/Golden Compass* 183) – is foregrounded by MacDonald in his essay "The Fantastic Imagination"; it is characteristic not only of German Romanticism but also of postmodernism[xxvi]. Both Pullman and MacDonald have been linked with both "movements" (or climates of thought and sensibility). Pullman's qualified alignment with postmodernism was noted above. The claim has also been made by various critics that MacDonald in some ways anticipated postmodernism[xxvii] (this should not surprise us, given Andrew Bowie's claim that in certain crucial respects German Romanticism anticipated postmodernism by well over a century). The considerable debt of MacDonald to *German* Romanticism is very well known; we need look no further than the epigraphs to *Phantastes*, and especially those by Novalis. Pullman too has a nostalgia for German Romanticism (as he has 'cheerfully' admitted in personal correspondence). For example, the list of "Works consulted and ideas stolen from" at the end of Pullman's *Count Karlstein or The Ride of the Deman Huntsman* includes "Caspar David Friedrich, *various pictures*" as well as Carl Maria von Weber's archetypal Romantic opera *Der Freischütz*, from which the plot of *Count Karlstein* is largely derived. *Count Karlstein* as well as *Clockwork* simply exude German Romanticism in general and E.T.A. Hoffmann in particular. Similar MacDonald tales would be "The Cruel Painter" and the tale of another Prague student, Cosmo von Wehrstahl, located at the centre of *Phantastes*.

The debt of both MacDonald and Pullman to *English* Romanticism is also evident. MacDonald was deeply interested in Wordsworth and Coleridge, as well as in Blake (though the extent of his knowledge of Blake is unclear). Pullman of course has declared himself of Blake's party, though the general Romantic attempt to re-imagine religious experience in a non-dogmatic and non-supernatural way clearly informs his work, as it also does that of MacDonald[xxviii]. Pullman has declared the importance to him of his traditional Anglican background; however, his evident love of Milton and Blake align him with the tradition of English dissent. MacDonald also came from a tradition of dissent, though the Congregationalist tradition to which he belonged tended to be dominated by Calvinist theology, with its 'puritanical martinet of a God' (Raeper, *MacDonald* 242). MacDonald not only aligned himself with the Christian Platonist tradition going back to Plotinus and Origen (also a universalist); he was also willing to explore the current of Gnosticism implicit in it (Raeper, *MacDonald* 240; 243; 257-8). That tradition included Boehme and Novalis, as well as more exotic writers such as Swedenborg, whom Blake memorably, if ambivalently, dismissed in *The Marriage of Heaven Hell*. MacDonald's predilection for the Wise Woman or Great-great-grandmother motif has also been widely seen as connected with the Sophia figure in Gnosticism[xxix].

Pullman too admits to an interest in Gnosticism, citing as a source Harold Bloom's novel *The Flight to Lucifer: a Gnostic Fantasy*, and raising the question of Gnosticism in his dialogue with Rowan Williams (Haill 87). But even if the oracle himself had not announced it, the Gnostic influence in 'His Dark Materials' would have been clearly evident. Pullman's so-called atheism could be seen as a Gnostic anti-theology in which, like some early Gnostics, he re-tells the Genesis story backwards; in this counter-version, the Fall is really an advance in human potential enabled by good offices of the serpent, the bringer of wisdom, who succeeds in circumventing the usurped power of the demiurge who is not the true God at all but merely the jealous creator of a shameful and imprisoning world[xxx]. The anti-clerical, anti-hierarchical and in some cases anti-patriarchal elements that inform historical Gnosticism reappear in Pullman's work. Above all, there seems to have been in historical Gnosticism a commitment to the power of stories narrating spiritual experience: 'Every one of them generates something new every day ... for no-one is considered initiated [or: 'mature'] among them unless he develops some enormous fictions', complained St Irenaeus (Pagels 48). The development of 'enormous fictions' intended to mediate spiritual insight could certainly be seen as characteristic of both Pullman and MacDonald. Both *Lilith* and 'His Dark Materials' are by any reckoning enormous in scope, comparable, *mutatis mutandis*, with David Lindsay's *Voyage to Arcturus* or perhaps Goethe's *Faust* - MacDonald himself apparently nursed the ambition to see *Lilith* compared to a kind of modern *Divine Comedy* (Raeper, *MacDonald* 367-9). Lewis's 'Space Trilogy' also seems to belong in this family constellation. Whether, or how, Lewis's other work might fit into this family group is a matter for discussion. Presumably Pullman would disown Lewis, but as I have argued above, a bit of internecine Oedipal conflict or misreading *à la* Bloom is only to be expected. And as I have suggested elsewhere (Gray, *Lewis* 45-6), Lewis's Christian Platonism comes much closer to Gnosticism (especially in the 'Space Trilogy') than one might expect, given the appropriation of his work by the orthodox. In this too, Lewis seems actually closer to the spirit of MacDonald than even his own more orthodox pronouncements might suggest.

Postscript

Who George MacDonald "misreads", and who his literary father-figure might be, is another question. At the beginning of *Phantastes*, Anodos's fairy grandmother is dismissive of his knowledge of his male precursors, and chides his ignorance of his female relatives; great-grandmothers and sisters are more to the point (MacDonald, *Phantastes* 5). The great-grandmother/Wise Woman motif is a marked feature of MacDonald's work, and can be interpreted as indicating MacDonald's interest in *pre-oedipal* maternal material (as I have argued in an article offering a Kristevan reading of *Phantastes*[xxxi]). Whether MacDonald's reliance on Novalis and the Sophia myth may suggest a different scenario than Bloom's aggressively Oedipal one, and whether this may allow a way to circumvent the Eve versus Lilith double-bind, predicated on what Gilbert and Gubar call, following Virginia Woolf, 'Milton's bogey' (Gilbert and Gubar 187-95) remains, I think, an open question. Behind the double misreading of Lewis by Pullman, and MacDonald by Lewis, there might be a link between MacDonald's and Pullman's attempts to get beyond the power nexus of patriarchal binary thinking. Such a link would have much to do with the subterranean connections of Romanticism and postmodernism, with both of which "movements' (or "styles" or "structures of sensibility") both MacDonald and Pullman have been associated.[xxxii]

Works Cited

Bloom, Harold. *The Anxiety of Influence*. New York: Oxford UP, 1973.
—. *A Map of Misreading*. New York: Oxford UP, 1975.
—. *The Flight to Lucifer: a Gnostic Fantasy,* New York: Farrar, 1979.
—. "*Clinamen*: Towards a Theory of Fantasy." Slusser, E., Rabkin, E. and Scholes, R., eds., *Bridges to Fantasy*. Carbondale: Southern Illinois UP, 1982.
Bowie, Andrew. *Aesthetics and Subjectivity: From Kant to Nietzsche*. 2nd ed. Manchester: Manchester UP, 2003.
Gilbert, Sandra M., and Gubar, Susan. *The Madwoman in the Attic*. New Haven: Yale UP, 1979.
Gray, William. *C.S. Lewis*. Plymouth: Northcote House (Writers and their Work), 1998.
—. "George MacDonald, Julia Kristeva and the Black Sun." *Studies in English Literature 1500-1900* (Autumn, 1996): 877-93.
Haill, Lyn, ed. *Darkness Illuminated*. London: National Theatre / Oberon Books, 2004.
Knoepflmacher, U.C., ed. *George MacDonald: The Complete Fairy Tales*. Harmondsworth: Penguin, 1999.
Leitch, Vincent, et al., eds., *The Norton Anthology of Theory and Criticism*. New York: Norton, 2001.
Lenz, Millicent with Scott, Carole, eds. *His Dark Materials Illuminated*. Detroit: Wayne State UP, 2005.
Lewis, C.S. *George MacDonald: An Anthology*. London: Bles, 1946.
—. *The Last Battle*. London: HarperCollins, 1997.
—. *Surprised by Joy*. London: Fontana, 1959.

—. *An Experiment in Criticism*. Cambridge: Cambridge UP, 1961.
MacDonald, George. *Phantastes: A Faërie Romance*. London: Dent (Everyman), 1915.
—. *Lilith*. Grand Rapids: Eerdmans, 1981.
—. ed. R. McGillis. *The Princess and the Goblin* and *The Princess and Curdie*. Oxford: Oxford UP, 1990.
Myers, Doris T. *C.S.Lewis in Context*. Kent State UP, 1994.
Pagels, Elaine. *The Gnostic Gospels*. Harmondsworth: Penguin, 1981.
Otto, Rudolf. *The Idea of the Holy*. Trans. John W. Harvey. 2nd ed. Oxford: Oxford UP, 1950.
Pullman, Philip. *Northern Lights* (= *The Golden Compass*). London: Scholastic, 1995.
Pullman, Philip. *Clockwork*. London: Corgi Yearling, 1997.
—. *Count Karlstein or The Ride of the Deman Huntsman*. London: Corgi Yearling, 1998.
Pullman, Philip. *The Amber Spyglass*. London: Scholastic, 2000.
William Raeper. *George MacDonald*. Tring: Lion, 1987.
—. ed. *The Gold Thread: Essays on George MacDonald*. Edinburgh: Edinburgh UP, 1990.
Rayment-Pickard, Hugh. *The Devil's Account: Philip Pullman and Christianity*. London: DLT, 2004.
Squires, Claire. *Philip Pullman's His Dark Materials' Trilogy*. London: Continuum, 2004.
Thacker, Deborah Cogan, and Webb, Jean. *Introducing Children's Literature: from Romanticism to Postmodernism*. London: Routledge, 2002.

[viii] Barbara Johnson's 'The Frame of Reference', which has been reprinted in various collections, first appeared in the special issue on 'Literature and Psychoanalysis' of *Yale French Studies* 55/56, 1977.

[ix] Erica Wagner, quoted in Claire Squires, *Philip Pullman's His Dark Materials' Trilogy* (London: Continuum, 2004) 74.

[x] Pullman has said in a discussion with Rowan Williams that he is "temperamentally ... 'agin' the postmodernist position that there is no truth and it depends on where you are and it's all the result of the capitalist, imperialist hegemony of bourgeois ... all this sort of stuff". See Lyn Haill, ed., *Darkness Illuminated* (London: National Theatre / Oberon Books, 2004) 101.

[xi] Philip Pullman, "The Dark Side of Narnia", *The Guardian,* October 1, 1998; quoted Squires 17.

[xii] See "The Little Girl Lost" in *Songs of Innocence.*

[xiii] Wendy Parsons and Catriona Nicholson, "Talking to Philip Pullman: An Interview", *The Lion and the Unicorn.*23:1 January 1999; quoted Squires 17.

[xiv] Pullman interview with Susan Roberts for Christian Aid, quoted Rayment-Pickard.45.

[xv] On Augustine, Platonism and Manichaeism see above all Peter Brown, *Augustine of Hippo* (London: Faber, 1967)
[xvi] See also the chapter "The Quest for Joy (or the Dialectic of Desire)" in Gray, *Lewis* 4-16.
[xvii] Personal correspondence with Philip Pullman.
[xviii] It is interesting to note how Bloom tries to transfer Lewis's ambivalent reading of MacDonald to his own equally ambivalent reading of Lindsay (Bloom, *Clinamen* 17).
[xix] See Lewis's inaugural lecture at Cambridge University where he presented himself as "Old Western Man" ("De Descriptione Temporum.", *Selected Literary Essays*); see also Gray, *Lewis* 2.
[xx] See, for example, James Monaco, *How to read a film : language, history, theory*, 3rd ed. (Oxford: Oxford UP, 2000).
[xxi] Since writing the above I have come across the following comment by Adelheid Kegler which seems to be saying something very similar: "Lewis klassifiziert MacDonald als guten Mythopoeten, jedoch eher mittelmässigen Schriftsteller ... Leider wird dieser Klassifizierung in der MacDonald-Literatur häufig noch unhinterfragt übernommen" ("Lewis classifies MacDonald as a good creator of myth, but as an average writer ... Unfortunately this classification is often taken on uncritically in writing on MacDonald"). Adelheid Kegler, "Einhundert Lichtjahre in neunzehn Stunden: Das rätselhafte Raumschiff in David Lindsay's *A Voyage to Arcturus*", *Inklings-Jahrbuch* 21 (2003) 162n4.
[xxii] See George MacDonald, *Lilith* (Eerdmans, 1981), p. 107, where "Samoil" (probably to be identified with "Sammael") is the name of the Shadow. 'Sammael' is also related to the Satanic figure of "Zamiel" who appears in Pullman's *Count Karlstein or The Ride of the Demon Huntsman*, and is derived from Carl Maria von Weber's opera *Der Freischütz*.
[xxiii] On MacDonald and Kristeva, see William Gray, "George MacDonald, Julia Kristeva and the Black Sun," *Studies in English Literature 1500-1900,* Autumn, 1996.
[xxiv] See for example Marcel Raymond, *From Baudelaire to Surrealism* (London: Methuen, 1970).
[xxv] See child_lit LISTERV (July 27, 2000). Also cited in Millicent Lenz with Carole Scott, eds., *His Dark Materials Illuminated* (Detroit: Wayne State UP, 2005) 5-6.
[xxvi] See, for example, Andrew Bowie, *Aesthetics and Subjectivity: From Kant to Nietzsche*, 2nd ed. (Manchester: Manchester UP, 2003) 8-15.
[xxvii] On MacDonald and postmodernism see Roderick McGillis, ed., *The Princess and the Goblin* and *The Princess and Curdie* (Oxford: Oxford UP, 1990) xvi-xxviii; Stephen Prickett in William Raeper, ed., *The Gold Thread* (Edinburgh: Edinburgh UP, 1990) 123-4; and Deborah Thacker and Jean Webb, *Introducing Children's Literature : from Romanticism to Postmodernism* (London: Routledge, 2002) 42-4; 140-2.
[xxviii] See for example M. H. Abrams, *Natural supernaturalism* (New York : Norton, 1973).
[xxix] See for example Deidre Hayward, "The Mystical Sophia: More on the Great Grandmother in the Princess Books", *North Wind: Journal of the George MacDonald Society*, 13, 1994.
[xxx] This summary of some key motifs in Gnosticism is dependent on, *inter alia*: Hans

Jonas, *The Gnostic Religion*, 2nd revised ed. (Boston : Beacon Press, 1963); James. M. Robinson, ed., *The Nag Hammadi Library in English* (Leiden : Brill, 1977); Elaine Pagels, *The Gnostic Gospels* (Harmondsworth: Penguin, 1981); Kurt Rudolph, *Gnosis* (Edinburgh : T. & T. Clark, 1983); Bentley Layton, ed., *The Gnostic scriptures : a new translation with annotations and introductions* (London : SCM, 1987); Giovanni Filoramo, *A History of Gnosticism* (Oxford: Blackwell, 1990).

[xxxi] See note 16.

[xxxii] A slightly different version of this essay appeared in *Mythlore* in 2007.

Chapter Seven

Voice, Gender and Alterity in George MacDonald's Fairy Tales

Maria Nikolajeva

Heterology, or discourse on the Other (de Certeau 1986), encompasses a number of theories dealing with unequal power positions in real life as well as in literature. While feminist theory has made us aware of male authors creating women characters as "the other", and while postcolonial theory reveals alterity in the images of ethnicity, a heterological approach to juvenile's literature would examine the power balance between the adult author and the implied young audience, which most tangibly manifests itself in the relationship between the ostensibly adult narrative voice and the child focalizing character and its perception of the fictive world. In other words, the way the adult narrator narrates the child reveals the degree of alterity – I say "degree", since alterity is by definition inevitable in writing for children. However, there are other factors besides age-related cognitive discrepancy in children's literature, which may both enhance and diminish the effect of power imbalance. I aim to look into some strategies of alterity in MacDonald's texts and consider the synergy of their impact on our perception.

To begin with, MacDonald operates within a non-mimetic mode, alternatively referred to in scholarship as fantasy or fairy tale, which is of no significance for my purpose. Rather, for practical reasons, I will henceforth refer to the two works for adults, *Phantastes* (1858) and *Lilith* (1895), as fantasies, and works for children, including full-lengths novels, as fairy tales.

It is well-known what MacDonald himself stated about the use of fantastic mode (MacDonald 1984); we must agree that his choice of mode and genre was conscious and deliberate, and that his models were the great German Romantic writers. Although MacDonald was undoubtedly a part of the Victorian fantasy tradition (Manlove 1975; Prickett 1979; Knoepflmacher 1998), his contemporary literature in Britain also developed along several other lines. In juvenile literature, we find both the exotic adventure of Rider Haggard, R.M. Ballantyne and G.A. Henty; and the didactic realism of *Tom Brown's*

Schooldays. MacDonald's exclusive use of non-mimetic modes is a strategy aimed at the utmost estrangement of the experience of the fictive characters from that of the narratee and the implied reader, may it be adult or young. I refrain from speculations about possible reasons, intentions and impacts, since this has been extensively examined before.

In MacDonald's fantasy novels, there are two worlds, the "real" fictional world of the protagonists/narrators and the dreamworld, or Faerie world, which they enter in a variety of ways. In Tzvetan Todorov's classification of non-mimetic writing (Todorov 1973), MacDonald's fantasies would fall within the category of the pure fantastic, since neither the characters nor the readers can ever be certain whether the events described are actually happening in the "real" fictional world or are the products of the characters' imagination, dreams, hallucinations or nightmares. The fantasies have often been called "dream romances", and their events and images have been treated either allegorically (Prickett 1979) or psychoanalytically (Jackson 1981).

Most of the fairy tales, marvellous in Todorov's sense, are less ambiguous. As soon as the central characters are princesses, the detached fairy-tale chronotope is evoked. *The Light Princess* opens in the conventional fairy-tale topos "Once upon a time" (15[xxxiii]) and an imaginary kingdom, a convention that the narratee is supposed to share. Let us remember that the original context of this particular story, the adult novel *Adela Cathcart* (1862), allows the narrator and the narratees to interact, and at one point the narratee comments on the credibility of the story. The setting is thus firmly removed from the narratee's experience. Similarly, *The Giant's Heart* begins: "There was once a giant who lived on the borders of Giantland..." (81). The time, place and the supernatural character create a sense of detachment, similar to Mikhail Bakhtin's description of the folktale chronotope (Bakhtin 1981). In *Cross Purposes*, there is a borderline between the real and the magic world, that can be traversed; yet the setting is again disconnected from the narratee:

> Once upon a time, the Queen of Fairyland, finding her own subjects far too well-behaved to be amusing, took a sudden longing to have a mortal or two at her court. (103)

In both cases, the story opens within the magic world, whereupon the ordinary children are brought into it. In *The Giant's Heart*, Tricksey-Wee merely walks into Giantland, looking for her lost brother, a well-known folktale motif. The crossing of the border is only marked by the change in size of the man-made objects: the giantess's thimble is as big as a bucket for Tricksey – an echo from *Gulliver's Travels* and anticipating *Alice in Wonderland*.

In *Cross Purposes*, the narrator states that "[n]o mortal, or fairy either, can tell where Fairyland begins and where it ends. But somewhere on the borders of

Fairyland there was a nice country village" (104). To bring mortals into Fairyland, messengers, or magic agents, are needed, and the passage for both main characters is through water – perhaps an allusion to Charles Kingsley's *Water Babies;* more likely an archetypal image. In this fairy tale, MacDonald also introduces the temporal principle that many 20th-century fantasy writers, beginning with Edith Nesbit, adopted: that the adventure in Fairyland does not take any of the primary time: "...Alice ran in the back way, and reached her own room before any one had missed her" (119). This is not really consistent with the earlier statement that she and Richard have grown up in Fairyland; but this can be interpreted metaphorically, as spiritual and mental growth. The temporal pattern is otherwise the reverse of that in folktales, in which the hero spends three, alternatively seven days with the fairies, only to discover on return that thousands of years have passed in his own world. When Diamond feels that he has been at the back of the north wind "...years and years [...] a hundred years..." (*At the Back of the North Wind* 104), only seven days have passed in his real world. By suggesting that Fairyland has its own temporal as well as spatial dimension, MacDonald enhances the sense of estrangement.

The Golden Key is slightly different from the other short fairy tales since it does not as explicitly place the narrative at a distance, but on the contrary, makes it sound like everyday: "There was a boy who used to sit in the twilight and listen to his great-aunt's stories" (120). The twilight, however, suggests the liminal state,[xxxiv] just as other similar topoi such as solstice, midsummer, midwinter, and so on. The liminality is immediately confirmed by the precision of the setting, which we recognize from MacDonald's other fairy tales: "...their little house stood on the borders of Fairyland" (120). There seems to be no marker between the worlds, yet Fairyland is distinct from the boy's real world since things work differently in it, such as the rainbow is clearly more solid. Unlike *Cross Purposes*, this fairy tale does adhere to the traditional temporal pattern: while Tangle feels she has only been away from home a short time, three years pass in her own time; and while wandering through Fairyland, both Tangle and Mossy grow up and age, only to be rejuvenated in the bath offered by the Old Man of the Sea. Growing up and growing old is presented as a reversible process; or the magical bath can be viewed as a ritual death and rebirth. At the same time, this is the only fairy tale with a linear plot (see Nikolajeva 2000): rather than returning to their own world, the characters go further on to the country whence the shadows fall, and, the narrator adds, "by this time I think they must have got there" (144; cf Sheley 2004).

At the Back of the North Wind (1871) is obviously the most reality-based of MacDonald's fairy tales. Except for the episodes with North Wind, it is a realistic story much in Dickens' style, full of misery and social injustice. With its supernatural elements, it could be perceived as genuinely fantastic in

Todorov's sense, since the young protagonist truly feels hesitation as to the nature of his experience:

> [...] he could hardly believe it himself when he thought about it in the middle of the day, although when the twilight was once half-way on to night he had no doubt about it, at least for the first few days after he had been with [North Wind]. (47)

Observe that here again twilight is the liminal topos in which the fantastic becomes believable. The narrator never expresses any doubt, explicitly or implicitly, that Diamond's experience is real; yet nobody except Diamond can see North Wind or hear her voice, thus the experience seems to have no objective truth to it – within the frames of the fictive topos of course, and the narrative rather falls into the category of uncanny. Diamond's initial flights over London and to the sea with North Wind are, from the objective, outside viewpoint, his dreams or perhaps daydreams, which is amplified by North Wind's words: "...you must go to bed first. I can't take you till you're in bed. That's the law about the children" (53). Diamond's journey to the country behind the north wind can be interpreted as his feverish hallucinations. The narrator states that "[...] he could not quite satisfy himself whether the whole affair was not a dream which he had dreamed when he was a very little boy" (151). The hesitation sustains almost to the end of the story; after a long time has passed since Diamond has seen North Wind, he begins to mistrust once again: "So strong did this feeling become, that at last he began to doubt whether he was not in one of those precious dreams..." (316). The inserted fairy tales are explicitly presented either as the characters' actual dreams ("Diamond's Dream", "Nanny's Dream") or as a hyponarrative ("Little Daylight").

Note that princess Irene in *The Princess and the Goblin* (1872) also feels recurrent doubts about the nature of her encounters with her great-great-grandmother: "Sometimes she came almost to the nurse's opinion that she had dreamed..." (32); "'Then it must all be a dream,' said Irene. 'I half thought it was; but I couldn't be sure. Now I am sure of it'" (76); "'...Please, I thought you were a dream...'" (81); "...even now she could not feel quite sure that she had not been dreaming" (95); "She grew frightened once more, thinking, that [...] the old lady might be a dream after all" (100). Since nobody can see the grandmother except Irene, just as nobody can see North Wind, it is natural to interpret the beautiful spinning-lady as a product of Irene's imagination and thus classify the story as uncanny. (We can also perceive her as an allegory, which in Todorov's view totally disqualifies the text as fantastic). However, in the sequel, *The Princess and Curdie* (1883), the young miner is also given the privilege of meeting the grand Progenitrix, the subjective experience thus giving way for a more objective one, and the narrative leaning toward marvellous rather than uncanny.

In any case, the choice of mode is MacDonald's foremost way of estrangement, since the characters are always honoured in being able to transcend the border of Otherworld.

The second strategy I would like to explore is MacDonald's choice of child protagonists. The fairy tales have been generally classified as addressed to children, and no controversy similar to the status of *Alice in Wonderland* has occurred around them. It is not my purpose to discuss whether the fairy tales are children's books or not; they have undeniably functioned as such, although I personally doubt that many children, or many adults for that part, appreciate the intricate dimensions of, for instance, *The Golden Key*. I will, however, keep to my own issues.

In the fantasies, MacDonald employs adult protagonists, while the fairy tales portray children. In this, MacDonald is not different from many other Romantic fantasy writers; for instance, his German model E. T. A. Hoffmann, whose *Nutcracker* is considered – at least outside the Anglo-Saxon criticism – as the very first fantasy novel written explicitly for children, while all his other works are addressed to adults; or the numerous Russian Romantic writers, who wrote for both audiences. In all these cases, the plots are somewhat similar, preferably featuring a quest, often combined with mysterious, weird experience. The difference lies not so much in the complexity, but in the first place in the adult issues, not least erotic ones. It is sufficient to compare the innocent world of toys in *Nutcracker* and the eerie world of automatons in *The Sandman*.

Among MacDonald's works, especially *Lilith* has distinct erotic subtones. It is, however, problematic, as always, to decide whether certain stories have been perceived and thus marketed as children's stories because they have young protagonists, or whether the author consciously addressed the young audience and therefore chose protagonists of suitable age (MacDonald does of course mention "my child readers" (99) in *At the Back of the North Wind*). Yet this circular argument is fruitless. We may also remember that children's literature was in MacDonald's time hardly as tangibly separate from the mainstream as it is today, and many books that we today label as children's were aimed at family reading. Of course, using a child protagonist as a symbol of innocence is the very essence of Romantic tradition, as is the close association of childhood and imagination. Yet can it also be that MacDonald, after the experience of writing *Phantastes*, chose child protagonists to avoid or circumvent the inevitable erotic aspects of dream narratives? In fact, in *The Light Princess*, his first children's story, published separately in 1864, the protagonist is seventeen, that is, of marriageable age, and indeed the story has quite explicit erotic scenes, as we know, strongly criticized by MacDonald's contemporaries. On the other hand,

Anodos in *Phantastes* is twenty-one, and Mr Vane has "just finished [his] studies at Oxford"; so the difference is not that great.

The age of the children in *Cross Purposes* is not stated, but as they fall in love with each other, the sexual aspect is immediately added. It is then explicitly stated they "seemed to have grown quite man and woman in Fairy-land" (119), which is reminiscent of the ending of Hans Christian Andersen's *The Snow Queen*. Also Tangle and Mossy in *The Golden Key* are children at the beginning of the story; Tangle is ten as she starts from home and thirteen as she arrives at the fairy's cottage: the change is significant since she is then a young woman rather than a little girl. At the end of the story, after having grown old and then young again, the characters are definitely adults.

Princess Irene is eight "at the time my story begins..." (*The Princess and the Goblin* 11), says the narrator, and continues: "...but she got older very fast" (12). Curdie is twelve and, as a working-class boy, he almost counts as an adult.

It is never mentioned explicitly how old Diamond is, but the narrator points out that Nanny, who earns her living by sweeping crossings, "was not really a month older than he was; only she had to work for her bread, and that so soon makes people older" (*North Wind* 45). In a coachman's family, a boy would likely be sent to earn his living by the age of seven, although probably not to drive a coach on his own, as Diamond eventually does. Everybody seems to think that he is too young to work.

Since MacDonald lets several characters repeatedly, in a variety of ways, suggest that Diamond is a halfwit, and also demonstrates the boy's naïve way of reasoning, the character is created as superficially inferior to his surrounding, what Northrop Frye calls ironic (Frye 1957). At the same time, Diamond's extreme goodness, kindness, intrinsic wisdom and impeccable morals give him almost mythic dimensions, and the privilege of having been at the back of the north wind, whatever meaning we may put into this assertion, makes him indeed exceptional. He is repeatedly referred to as a "God's baby", which, even stripped of its direct Christian meaning, suggests a common belief in the parity of madness and sanctity. Dostoyevsky's Prince Myshkin is a good example; yet in Diamond's case, his being a child adds an overall sense of innocence to the image. No matter how the readers perceive and interpret the protagonist, the subjectivity offered by the text is indisputably displaced from Diamond.

MacDonald here uses the child as a symbol, or archetype, in the Jungian sense; as a bearer of ideology and ethics rather than a human character. Not surprisingly, then, MacDonald eventually gives Diamond a slightly more earthbound adult double, Mr Raymond, who is a poet, even though he has not been at the back of the north wind. Here, MacDonald equals Diamond's sacrosanct insanity with the adult's creativity. Mr Raymond recognizes this, saying: "'I suspect the child's a genius [...] and that's what makes people think him silly'" (186). In "Diamond's Dream", his celestial origin is hinted at, which puts him in the long row of "alien children", once again going back to MacDonald's favourite model E. T. A. Hoffmann and his second children's book, *Das fremde Kind* (1818).[xxxv] In other words, Diamond is a magic agent in a plot that, paradoxically, lacks a hero, unless we can count the little sweeping-girl Nancy, whom he helps, as a hero. Alternatively, Mr Raymond or indeed the anonymous narrator can be interpreted as the true protagonists of the novel, while Diamond is their "inner child", in the same sense that the pilot-narrator is the true protagonist of *The Little Prince*, a much later "alien-child" story.

It has been repeatedly pointed out that MacDonald claimed to have a special power of addressing children, the notorious "for the childlike" (McGillis 1992); however, we need yet to take a closer look at the texts to decide whether there is indeed a single child address in them. Rather I would say that they have, as most contemporary Victorian works, double address in which adult co-readers can find levels of meaning to their own satisfaction, whether allegorical or psychological. MacDonald definitely does not employ the dual address, or "the twentieth-century voice", as Barbara Wall names it, characteristic of his close successor Edith Nesbit (Wall 1991). MacDonald never goes down to the child's level of perception, never takes the child's part. The child in the fairy tales is and remains "the other", the perfect image of lost and irretrievable purity. We can of course maintain that some stories, not least *The Light Princess*, do involve the dilemma of growing up and acquiring gravity in more than one sense, thus prefiguring *Peter Pan*. Yet the adult experience is treated in a casual fairy-tale manner similar to "happily ever after", in *The Light Princess* somewhat more elaborate: "... the prince and princess lived and were happy, and had crowns of gold, and clothes of cloth, and shoes of leather, and children of boys and girls..." (53).

Whatever the reason for choosing child characters, they are narrated from an unequal power balance, whether the opposition is simply: adult – child, or the more intricate and psychologically complex: experience – innocence. While the literal point of view in, for instance, *The Princess and the Goblin*, might be that of Irene, the narrator persistently refers to her as "the little princess" and mentions her "little head" (19), or "little feet" (80), a typical example of talking down to children, which immediately creates a discrepancy between the "childlike" point of view and the adult, detached voice (similarly, I must say to the use of the word "child" about Tangle as well as Diamond and Nanny). In this, MacDonald is no different from any other writer for children. What can differ is the degree in which the adult writers manage to subvert their own power position and empower the fictive child. It seems that MacDonald has no intention whatsoever of being subversive in this respect. The subjectivity of his texts lies firmly with the adult narrator, and child characters are merely instrumental to his purposes.

This brings me to the next aspect of my investigation, that of narrative perspective. In adult fantasies MacDonald chooses personal narration, which brings their experience as close to the reader as can be. In the fairy tales, by contrast, the narration is, like in most 19th-century children's books, what normally is called impersonal, or third-person. I say "normally", since the narrator frequently makes himself explicitly present in the text as a voice, and, in *At the Back of the North Wind*, even makes the child protagonist's acquaintance. Yet, this apparent metafictional trait rather enhances the distance between the narrator and the narratee. Although appearing in flesh and blood in Chapter 35 of the story, the anonymous "I" has otherwise all the features ascribed to the omniscient narrator of the traditional fairy tales. Let us consider the famous beginning of the book:

> I have been asked to tell you about the back of the North Wind. An old Greek writer mentions a people who lived there [...] My story is not the same as his. I do not think Herodotus had got the right account of the place. I am going to tell you how it fared with a boy who went there. (7)

First of all, the narrator has a clear and self-confident voice, and he claims to have knowledge and authority beyond the ordinary. The source of his information is Diamond, who by all means should be perceived as unreliable. When Diamond eventually gets to the country at the back of the north wind, the narrator admits his incapacity to deal with it:

> I have now come to the most difficult part of my story. And why? Because I do not know enough about it. And why should I not know as much about this part as about any other part? for of course I could know nothing about the story except Diamond had told it; and why should not Diamond tell about the country at the back of the north wind, as well as about his adventures in getting there? Because, when he came back, he had forgotten a great deal. And what he did remember was very hard to tell. (96)

At this point, Chapter 10, the narrator has yet not disclosed how he has gained access to Diamond's story, saying that "Diamond never told these things to anyone but – no, I had better not say who it was, but whoever it was told me..." (99). As it turns out, the mysterious person is the narrator himself, which, however, is not revealed until almost the very end of the story. Seeing Diamond's lifeless body, the narrator concludes: "They thought he was dead. I knew he had gone to the back of the north wind" (332). As the narrator by this time has established himself as homodiegetic, that is, a material part of his own fictive world, we can only perceive this statement as his belief, not as an ultimate truth. However, also the less perceptible narrator of *The Golden Key* concludes his story by a supposition about the fate of his characters. This ambivalent position of the narrator contributes to the complexity of some of the stories.

In most of the fairy tales the narrator is straightforwardly omniscient and shifts easily between the characters, including the evil ones, for instance, the bad fairy in *The Light Princess*, revealing her wicked plans of draining the lake. The narrator emphasizes his exclusive omnipresence by saying: "If any one had followed the witch-princess, he would have heard her unlock exactly one hundred doors..." (41). He can enter people's minds: "I cannot tell whether Diamond knew what she was thinking, but I think I know" (*North Wind* 116); or "[Mr Raymond] had meant to test Joseph when he made the bargain about Ruby" (291). As omniscient, the narrator can see into the future, in form of prolepses, for instance, the explanation why princess Irene is not allowed to go out after dark: "... they had good reasons, as we shall see by and by" (*The Princess and the Goblin* 14); or "...when I have informed [my readers] concerning what Curdie learned the very next night, they will be able to understand" (50).

Omniscience also includes omnipresence and effortless switching between different places of action: "And now I will go back to the borders of the forest" (123); "Meanwhile Mossy had got out of the lake..." (141); "Now while [Diamond] is lying there, getting strong again with chicken broth and other nice things, I will tell my readers what had been taking place at his home, for they ought to be told it" (*North Wind* 109); "Diamond set off, never suspecting that the policeman, who was a kind-hearted man, with children of his own, was following him close..." (178).

The narrator repeatedly underscores his authority that enables him to have access to knowledge unattainable to other mortals: "...nobody even knew she was a fairy, except the other fairies" (*North Wind* 227). While this of course is the common convention of fictionality, the narrator accentuates his special knowledge of events, such as: "Once upon a time, so long ago that *I have quite forgotten the date*..." (15; emphasis added); as well as characters, as in the description of the evil fairy: "What [her eyes] looked like when she loved anybody, I do not know; for I never heard of her loving anybody, but herself" (16). On the other hand, the statement "I may here remark that it was very amusing to see [the princess] run" (24) creates a sense that the narrator is corporeally present at the events described, which contradicts the setting of the story as "once upon a time". Similarly, when in *At the Back of the North Wind*, the narrator says: "It was great fun to see Diamond teaching [Nanny] how to hold the baby" (271), we may wonder whose literal point of view we are invited to share. It is exactly such tiny details that shatter the character-tied subjectivity.

In particular, the narrator almost boasts of his familiarity with the Fairyland and its ways. "I have seen this world – only sometimes, just now and then [...] – look as strange as ever I saw Fairyland. But I confess that I have not seen Fairyland at its best" (20). We may assume that the narrator has a first-hand experience of the Fairyland, similar to that of Anodos and Mr Vane.

Occasionally the narrator accounts for this authority: "I refer any one who doubts this part of my story to certain chronicles of Giantland preserved among the Celtic nations" (85). The motif of a giant or ogre whose heart is preserved outside his body is common in folktales all over the world, so to an informed reader this statement may sound ironic; once again, *The Giant's Heart* was originally told by a hypodiegetic narrator Mr Smith in *Adela Cathcart* to a group of young listeners.

There are quite a few typical features that MacDonald's intrusive narrator shows. He is free to pass judgements on the character, such as: "She was, *indeed*, a very nice queen..." (15; emphasis added); "...it was *no wonder* that her brother forgot her..." (16); "[The princess] never could be brought to see the serious side of anything" (23); "She was perfectly obstinate" (29); "The *poor* princess nearly went out of *the little mind she had*" (39); "... [Diamond] was not frightened, for he had not yet learned how to be..." (*North Wind* 10); "...[Diamond] thought he had been of no use to her. He was mistaken there..." (44); "...Mr Raymond was one of the kindest men in London" (182); "...she was as brave as could be expected of a princess her age" (*The Princess and the Goblin* 17), and so on.

Further, the narrator shows metafictional awareness of the genre, as he says: "Of course somebody was forgotten", missed from the invitation list for the christening in *The Light Princess* (16). Interestingly enough, in *Little Daylight*, the narrator is just as conscious of the genre, as he comments: "...I never knew of any interference on the part of a wicked fairy that did not turn out a good thing in the end" (228). Taken separately, the story may then seem to have exactly the same intrusive narrator as the other fairy tale; in its original context, chapter 28 of *At the Back of the North Wind*, it is told by Mr Raymond to the children at the hospital, so that the comment on genre has its very concrete narratees.

The narrator repeatedly employs direct address (which can naturally also be perceived as rhetorical questions): "...poor relations don't do anything to keep you in mind of them. Why don't they? The king could not see into the garret [his sister] lived in, could he?" (16); or "What do you think she saw? A very old lady who sat spinning" (*The Princess and the Goblin* 19). Many of the similar remarks have the function of creating an intimate, conversational tone, quite common in 19th-century children's literature: "Now, as I have already said..." (*North Wind* 9). Besides, the readers are invoked in phrases such as: "It is plain enough to every one of my readers..." (*The Princess and the Goblin* 97); "...lest my reader should have his qualms... I venture to remind him..." (*North Wind* 177); "My readers will not wonder that [...] I did my very best to gain the friendship of Diamond" (312). One comment in *At the Back of the North Wind* is of a special significance for my purpose: "Now if any of my child readers want to know what a genius is – shall I try to tell them, or shall I not?" (186). The statement shows the narrator's distrust in – if not contempt toward young audience, amplified on the following page: "And if you do not understand that, I am afraid you must be content to wait till you grow older and know more" (187).

Irony is yet another means of displacing the narrator's subject position toward the character's, and thus the reader's:

> Whether the prince was so near perfection that he has a right to demand perfection itself, I cannot pretend to say. All I know is, that he was a fine, handsome, brave, generous, well-bred, and well-behaved youth, as all princes are. (31).

Also the following comment on narration is obviously meant to be ironic: "I won't vouch for what the old horse was thinking, for it is very difficult to find out what any old horse is thinking" (*North Wind* 147). Here the omniscient narrator suddenly admits his limit, although, within genre conventions, it would not be more remarkable for him to enter the mind of a horse than to enter the mind of a fairy. In fact, Diamond is later allowed to overhear the two horses' conversation.

Every now and then the narrator takes pain to account for the events he is describing: 'Her atrocious aunt had deprived the child of all her gravity. If you ask me how this was effected, I'd answer, "In the easiest way in the world. She had only to destroy gravitation"' (17). This explanation would probably leave a child reader puzzled, but gives the narrative voice a quasi-authority. On the other hand, the narrator can state that he cannot explain how gravity worked for the princess: "The exact preposition expressing this relation I do not happen to know" (25); or "Whether this was owing to the fact that water had been employed as the means of conveying the injury, I do not know" (29).

The fairy tales are not free from didacticism common for the 19th-century children's literature (but, I must remark, totally absent from MacDonald's fantasies). It may be a question of a single sentence, such as: "...the wearer of Grandmother's clothes never thinks how he or she looks, but thinks always how handsome other people are" (130) or "...I have observed that the most wonderful thing in the world is how people come to understand anything" (*North Wind* 21); but also the whole account of Mr Coleman's misfortunes in Chapter 12 of *At the Back of the North Wind* is a didactic sermon on virtue, as are reflections on self-praise in Chapter 16 and the story of the drunken cabman in Chapter 18.

Significant for the understanding of the narrator's function are his metafictional comments on the narrative process: "... in her laugh there was something missing. What is was, I find myself unable to describe" (24); "How long they were in crossing this plain I cannot tell" (133); "It is quite impossible for me to describe what he saw" (*North Wind* 63); "I must not go on describing what cannot be described..." (65); "What Mr Raymond thought, I dare hardly attempt to put down here" (296); "I will not describe the varied feelings of the party..." (296). Notably, the hypodiegetic narrator of "Little Daylight" repeatedly uses the same formula as the main narrator: "I will not attempt to describe what they had to go through..." (*North Wind* 230); "I shall not attempt to describe his misery..." (239). Such statements may be used to inspire the reader's imagination, but they also remind us of the narrator's constant presence. On a deeper level, they convey a writer's frustration, which is more evident in the fantasies, for instance, the much-quoted passage from Chapter 4 in *Phantastes*.

The most tangible illustrations of the narrator's awareness of his own narrative status are his repeated excuses for the liberties he takes with putting correct words to his young characters' experiences. Pondering on Diamond's memories of the country at the back of the north wind, he says: "I do not mean that he thought these very words. They are perhaps too grown-up for him to have thought, but they represent the kind of thing that was in his heart and his head" (*North Wind* 130). It is still more explicit in his dealing with Nanny's hyponarrative:

> My readers must not suppose that poor Nanny was able to say what she meant so well as I put it down here. She had never been to school, and had heard very little else than vulgar speech [...] But I have been to school, and [...] it has made me able to tell her dream better than she could herself. (253)

This, if anything, reveals the narrator's superior position toward the characters – as well as the readers, who ostensibly need an explanation of the conventions of fictive discourse. On a more sophisticated level, the narrator appeals to the child or the "childlike", who may not yet have mastered the language to perfection, and 'lends out his voice', to borrow a concept from postcolonial theory, to those who lack a voice of their own. Stephen Prickett calls MacDonald's struggle with language "a theological activity" (Prickett 1979, 176) and concludes that for MacDonald the inadequacy of language to convey a metaphysical experience is the very essence of fantasy. Jacques Lacan would refer to this dilemma as the tension between the imaginary and the symbolic. MacDonald's endeavour is thus to translate the imaginary into the symbolic, and as the imaginary is that of the child, the mission implies estranging the child from its natural way of experience. This is, I quite realize, a controversial stance that will need more exploration.

Yet it should be quite obvious from my discussion that the authoritative adult voice in MacDonald's fairy tales has a significantly stronger effect than the child characters' point of view. Unlike, for instance, Deborah Thacker, I do not see any invitation to child readers to participate in a dialogue on equal rights (Thacker and Webb 2002, 44). In my view, MacDonald's texts are monologically transmitted from the adult narrator to child narratees, whether overt or covert.

Besides, it is far from always that MacDonald actually uses his child characters as focalizers, and when he does, primarily external focalization is employed. It is here that I want to test my ideas about gender and alterity. One might expect that, being male, MacDonald would be more likely to reflect male protagonist's experiences more profoundly. In both adult fantasies, MacDonald chooses a male protagonist, which seems natural as he attempts to convey a subjective, emotionally charged experience of his characters' encounter with the Other (as I am not primarily dealing with the fantasies, I will not pursue this matter).

The intriguing feature of the fairy tales is the alternative uses of male and female protagonists, which is not as common as it may seem; in fact, statistically, male authors tend to choose male protagonists and female authors choose female protagonists. If we consider some of MacDonald's contemporaries, Charles Kingsley has a male protagonist in *Water Babies*, Mrs Molesworth has a female protagonist in *The Cuckoo Clock*, while Lewis Carroll has a female protagonist in the two *Alice* books. MacDonald's immediate successor, Edith Nesbit, introduced the multiple protagonist, a group of girls and boys, a device successfully circumventing the issue of gender.

Many scholars, notably Rod McGillis, have considered gender in MacDonald's works, however, from feminist-psychoanalytical rather than narrative premises (McGillis 2003); while others, like Deborah Thacker, have focused on the feminine, imaginary, in Lacanian terms, language (Thacker 2001). In approaching MacDonald, I assumed that heterofocalization, the use of a focalizer of the opposite gender, would involve different narrative devices than homofocalization; that is, the female children would be narrated in a different manner than male. My hypothesis was thus that MacDonald chose female characters in order to still further distance the narrating agency from the experiencing one (once again, contrary to the established views).

In her essay "Images of Evil", that I have previously quoted in a number of contexts, Nancy Veglahn proposes a psychoanalytical interpretation of heterofocalization (Veglahn 1987). Her thesis is that evil figures in fiction are based on the author's subconscious perception of evil as being of the opposite gender, a clear case of gender-related "othering". MacDonald is one of Veglahn's examples, alongside *Alice* books, *The Wizard of Oz* and the *Narnia* stories. She demonstrates further that to counterbalance the female monsters, male authors employ strong female characters, typically ascribed the Jungian function as the author's Anima.[xxxvi]

Far from subscribing to the psychoanalytical theory of literature, I nevertheless find Veglahn's patterns fascinating. Yet she has obviously neglected the fact that MacDonald employs both genders in his fairy tales (while, I may add, deviating from Veglahn's model in the fantasies, at least as far as the protagonist is concerned). Veglahn's paradigm of male author – female monster – female protagonist fits, besides her own examples, *The Princess and the Goblin* and *The Princess and Curdie*, subsequently examined from the Jungian point of view by Joseph Sigman (1992), also *The Light Princess* and *Little Daylight*.

We may perhaps consider the North Wind as a monster in the Jungian sense, as mysterious and ambivalent Other; however, she is at the same time the positive female principle, combining the Jungian archetypes of Anima and the Wise Old Woman. As to protagonist, Diamond is, at least superficially, male. This may seem a strange statement, as the character is definitely referred to as "a boy" and with the personal pronoun "he"; however, we have learned from recent critical theory that gender is a social construction, as well as that fictive children are literary constructions; gender in fiction is then part of characterization and can be constructed unrestricted by the limitations of biological sex. In a literary text the gendered features ascribed to characters and their gendered behaviour, or "performance" in Judith Butler's sense, are more important than their formal description as male or female.

If we, by way of mental exercise or narratological commutative test, change the protagonist's gender in *At the Back of the North Wind*, we will clearly see that no other major changes would be required. Perhaps some subtle erotic hint would be lost; yet the magnitude of the North Wind as the image of death surpasses her possible erotic attraction (unlike, one might add, the figure of Lilith). The story would, in other words, be viable with a female protagonist. In fact, Diamond is very much an androgynous figure, described as possessing many feminine traits, or, in Butler's words, performing feminine. MacDonald supports our general perception of Diamond as effeminate by several direct statements:

> He never touched any of the flowers or blossoms, for he was not like some boys who cannot enjoy a thing without pulling it to pieces, and so preventing everyone from enjoying it after them. (50)

Also his surroundings perceive him as feminine, as the cabmen say: "You're a plucky one, for all your girl's looks!" (195).

The Princess and the Goblin can be viewed as a feminine version of *At the Back of the North Wind*, with Irene meeting the monster who is at the same time a mentor. Likewise, a boy can be substituted for Irene without the story needing other substantial revisions. One could possibly argue that the spinning symbolism, connected to the feminine (see Jenkins 2004), would be lost; however, I feel that since it works just as well with Curdie, it still would be valid. It would seem then that children in MacDonald's fairy tales are more or less gender-neutral, generic "children" rather than boys and girls.

Let us take a closer look at heterofocalization in *The Light Princess*. In the chapters where the princess acts as a focalizer, her experience is based on the external senses: sight, sound, and in the first place, touch. She is depicted by the narrator as enjoying her weightlessness or the touch of the water; however, her inner emotions are never portrayed. One might argue that external focalization is normal in the 19th-century children's literature, yet it would seem that the author of *Phantastes* should not have problems with entering a character's mind. The choice of external focalization must then be deliberate and serve an artistic purpose. I see the purpose as contributing to othering. Moreover, rather than looking, the princess is looked at–by the prince, and not least by the narrator, with the notorious "male gaze" as well as the Victorian "child-eroticizing" gaze. Objectification is one of the foremost indications of alterity. When the prince first meets the princess, the scene is explicitly voyeuristic:

> Looking over the lake, he saw something white in the water... There was not light enough to show that she was a princess, but quite enough to show that she was a lady, for it does not want much light to see that. (32)

As the story progresses, the male rescuer – much like in traditional folktales - supersedes the female protagonist, sacrificing his life and becoming the hero. The Christian connotations of the sacrifice are obvious and have been repeatedly observed; and while some elements of parody are evident as well, the story turns out as a conventional female coming-of-age narrative in which the bewitched female has only to wait for the right male to save her. In fact, the prince's emotions, presented through simple quoted monologue (44), at least allow a glimpse of his inner life, views and morals. The princess, even though she gains gravity, remains completely flat as a character. Much the same happens in *Little Daylight*.

However, we may detect a similar strategy in the description of Diamond. On his journeys with North Wind, he is an observer: he looks, sees, espies, and so on, but very seldom reflects on what he sees. When he is travelling north, the landscape is described in what may be perceived as figural discourse, especially emphasized by the statement: "How long this lasted Diamond had no idea" (*North Wind* 89). But generally, Diamond is, as earlier proposed, an archetype rather than a real character.

The Princess and the Goblin suggests by its title that princess Irene is the protagonist, while the goblin is the antagonist (here I could argue with Nancy Veglahn whether it is indeed the goblin queen who is the main villain and the image of MacDonald's perverted perception of the opposite sex). Irene is focalized externally in slightly more than half of the chapters; the rest, with just a few exceptions, take on Curdie's point of view. Curdie has the helper function in the plot, but through focalization becomes almost as important as Irene. In the description of Irene and Curdie's escape through the underground tunnels, the most dramatic episode of the story, the point of view is switched back and forth between them. In the sequel, Curdie overrules Irene and becomes the hero, which is something we have observed both in folktales and in MacDonald's own fairy tales.[xxxvii] Thus *The Princess and the Goblin* in practice features a collective, or multiple protagonist, that also appears in *The Giant's Heart*, *Cross Purposes*, and *The Golden Key*, anticipating Edith Nesbit. However, while Nesbit most often has a group of children in the centre (emphasized by such titles as *Five Children and It* or *The Railway Children*), MacDonald presents a cross-gender *actant* consisting of a boy and a girl.

The Giant's Heart features the sister and brother, with the significant names of Tricksey-Wee and Buffy-Bob, who largely perform as a single *actant* in the story. Tricksey has perhaps a more substantial and active role; yet in the many versions of the folktale, on which *The Giant's Heart* is modelled, the trickster part can be played by a male as well as a female actor. In *Cross Purposes*, a class opposition is added to the gender one, as Alice is the daughter of a squire, and Richard the son of a poor widow, a conflict fully developed in *The Princess and the Goblin*. The pattern is common in folktales as well as popular romances of the time; MacDonald emphasizes the class difference by giving the children appropriate messengers who bring them to Fairyland: a pretty fairy for the girl and an ugly goblin for the boy. Although they initially get a chapter each, describing their separate passages into Fairyland, and although Alice is introduced first, she is in this fairy tale given the traditional role of the "princess" in Proppian sense, the object of the quest, devoid of agency, which is repeatedly emphasized as Alice bursts into tears while Richard comes with solutions, as well as statements such as: "…he caught up Alice in his *strong arms*…" (115; emphasis added). Richard also looks at Alice with the infamous "male gaze" as he discovers that he is in love. Prior to that, Alice has been presented, through the narrator's view, as spoilt and disagreeable. However, we get a glimpse of Alice's thoughts: "Can it be that I love the poor widow's son?" (115), and the two characters more or less amalgamate into one single actant with the common goal of getting back home. I will not here speculate in how MacDonald's gender construction could have been affected by having read the manuscript of *Alice in Wonderland*.[xxxviii]

The two children are equally objectified, presented as toys at the Fairy Queen's will. Their successful rite of passage notwithstanding, they are not united, but have to part, since class borders seem, unlike the borders of Fairyland, to be impenetrable. Instead, "[i]n reward of their courage, the Fairy Queen sent them permission to visit Fairy-land as often as they pleased" (119). This is an equivocal ending; as Fairyland in MacDonald's works may stand for dreamland as well as the realm of the dead, the young lovers are promised that they can only be together in their imagination or in death. By adding two short paragraphs about the fate of the fairy Peaseblossom and the goblin Toadstool, MacDonald definitely detaches the subject position of the text from the young protagonists. In other words, he feels quite indifferent about them and does not encourage the reader's empathy either.

In *The Golden Key*, contrary to *Cross Purposes*, the male character is introduced first. As he finds the golden key, the reader is encouraged to perceive him as the hero of the story and share his subjectivity. Interestingly enough, this strategy is partially undermined as he initially does not have a name and thus has a very vague identity, a motif that MacDonald develops in *Lilith* where the narrator forgets his name and loses his sense of identity as he enters Fairyland. At the same time, in *The Golden Key*, MacDonald comes conspicuously close to figural discourse, such as free indirect speech conveying the boy's ponderings upon the golden key: "Where was the lock to which the key belonged? It must be somewhere, for how could anybody be so silly as make a key for which there was no lock? Where should he go to look for it?" (122). Figural discourse creates a sense of intimacy and proximity to the character.

The female protagonist, who also initially has no name, is introduced as lacking agency, neglected and almost unpleasant, although the narrator stresses that it is not her fault. She is thus immediately put into an objectified position, and even though she is focalized externally, the omniscience of the narrator is constantly manifested: "...although she did not know it, this was the very best way she could have gone" (124). When the characters part on the quest, Tangle is given more room, but on the other hand, she has to go through more trials than Mossy, which not only shows that male and female initiation takes different forms, but also gives preference to the male as "the chosen" and leaves the passive role to the female: "Seven years had she sat there waiting" (143). While the story in many details shows striking similarities to Andersen's *The Snow Queen*, the gender performance of MacDonald's characters is the opposite of Andersen's.

My argument is supposed to show that in MacDonald's fairy tales, the child characters are exchangeable as far as gender is concerned, and when multiple protagonists are used, gender permutation is effective. MacDonald's choice of the protagonists' gender seems arbitrary, at least from the narratological point of view, and no significant difference between homofocalization and heterofocalization can be detected. Among many other details, the word "child", with the ambivalent undertones of admiration and condescension, is used about boys and girls indiscriminatively. Rod McGillis suggests that MacDonald is "queering" gender in his works, putting in the concept the original significance of "strange", "peculiar", "different" (McGillis 2003), by extension, Other. I would pursue the argument saying that MacDonald "queers" his protagonists, in the same sense, irrespective of gender; that a child in itself is "strange", "odd" and "different".

I have initially stated that the overall perception of power balance in a text would depend on a synergetic effect of the various aspects of alterity. It would seem, from my obviously limited investigation that the adult – child axis of the power tension is so significantly stronger than the gender axis that the latter is practically negligible. In their Kristevian/Lacanian readings of MacDonald, William Gray discusses (Gray 1996) and Ruth Jenkins develops (Jenkins 2004) the idea of "the precariousness of subject position" in MacDonald's works. I hope that my narratological examination supports this observation.

Works Cited

Bakhtin, Mikhail. "The Forms of Time and Chronotope in the Novel." In his *The Dialogic Imagination*. Austin: University of Texas Press, 1981, 84-258.
Certeau, Michel de. *Heterologies. Discourse on the Other*. University of Minnesota Press, 1986
Frye, Northrop. *Anatomy of Criticism. Four Essays*. Princeton: Princeton University Press, 1957.
Gray, William N. "George MacDonald, Julia Kristeva and the Black Sun". *Studies in English Literature: 1500-1900*. 36 (1996) 4: 877-93.
Jackson, Rosemary. *Fantasy: The Literature of Subversion*. New York: Methuen, 1981.
Jenkins, Ruth Y."'I am Spinning This for You, My Child': Voice and Identity Formation in George MacDonald's Princess Books". *The Lion and the Unicorn* 28 (2004) 3: 325-344.
Knoepflmacher, U. C. *Ventures into Childland. Victorians, Fairy Tales, and Femininity*. Chicago: The University of Chicago Press, 1998.
—. "Introduction". In: MacDonald, George. *The Complete Fairy Tales*. Edited by U. C. Knoepflmacher. London: Penguin, 1999, vii-xx.

MacDonald, George. *At the Back of the North Wind* [1871]. London: Penguin, 1984.
—. *The Complete Fairy Tales*. Edited by U. C. Knoepflmacher. London: Penguin, 1999.
—. "The Fantastic Imagination". In: *Fantasists on Fantasy*. Edited by R.H. Boyer and K. J. Zahorski. New York: Ballantine, 1984, 14-21.
—. *Lilith* [1895]. Grand Rapids, Mi: Eerdman, 2000.
—. *Phantastes* [1858]. New York: Ballantine, 1970.
—. The Princess and Curdie [1882]. London: Penguin, 1966.
—. The Princess and the Goblin [1872]. London: Penguin, 1964.
Manlove, C. N. *Modern Fantasy. Five Studies*. Cambridge: Cambridge University Press, 1975.
McGillis, Roderick. "A Fairytale is Just a Fairytale: George MacDonald and the Queering of Fairy". *Marvels & Tales* 17 (2003) 1: 86-99.
McGillis, Roderick, ed. *For the Childlike. George MacDonald's Fantasies for Children*. Metuchen, NJ: Scarecrow, 1992.
Nikolajeva, Maria. *From Mythic to Linear: Time in Children's Literature*. Lanham, Md: Scarecrow, 2000.
Prickett, Stephen. *Victorian Fantasy*. Hassocks: Harvester Press, 1979.
Sheley, Erin. "From Eden to Eternity: The Timescales of Genesis in George MacDonald's *The Golden Key* and *Lilith*." *Children's Literature Association Quarterly* 29 (2004) 4: 329-344.
Sigman, Joseph. "The Diamond in the Ashes. A Jungian Reading of the 'Princess' Books." In McGillis, Rod, ed. *For the Childlike. George MacDonald's Fantasies for Children*. Methuchen, NJ: Scarecrow, 1992: 183-194.
Thacker, Deborah. "Feminine Language and the Politics of Children's Literature". *The Lion and the Unicorn* 25 (2001) 1: 3-16.
Thacker, Deborah Cogan, and Jean Webb. *Introducing Children's Literature. From Romanticism to Postmodernism*. London: Routledge: 2002.
Todorov, Tzvetan. *The Fantastic: A Structural Approach to a Literary Genre*. Cleveland: The Press of Case Western Reserve University, 1973.
Veglahn, Nancy. "Images of Evil: Male and Female Monsters in Heroic Fantasy". *Children's literature* 15 (1987): 106-119.
Wall, Barbara. *The Narrator's Voice. The Dilemma of Children's Fiction*. London: Macmillan, 1991.

[xxxiii] Unless otherwise stated, all quotes are from *Complete Fairy Tales*.
[xxxiv] Cf Knoepflmacher, note 1 to "The Golden Key" in *Complete Fairy Tales*.
[xxxv] Some later figures with a similar role are, for instance, Antoine de Saint-Exupery's Little Prince, Maurice Druon's Tistou of the Green Thumbs, and Michael Ende's Momo.

[xxxvi] Veglahn would have received confirmation for her proposed patterns in the two recent texts, *His Dark Material* and *Harry Potter* books.
[xxxvii] Something similar happens in Burnett's *The Secret Garden*.
[xxxviii] The allusions to and direct quotations from *Alice* in *Cross Purposes*, including the name, have been noticed by Uli Knoepflmacher.

CHAPTER EIGHT

JOURNEYS INTO DARKNESS:
JOSEPH CONRAD'S *HEART OF DARKNESS*
AND GEORGE MACDONALD'S *LILITH*

ELMAR SCHENKEL

Joseph Conrad's short novel *Heart of Darkness* is one of the most famous, yet also most controversial works of modern English literature. I know of no other literary text that has so much been exposed to all kinds of re-writings, fictional responses or travelogues, from all corners of the world, let alone the growing mountain of criticism increasing by some hundred contributions a year.[xxxix] Every other journalist who makes a reference to the Congo these days (in 2006) does not forget to mention the metaphorical use of the "heart of darkness", a kind of condensation of the image of the "Black Continent"; everything, from politics to morals and skin colour seems to fit so nicely. Whatever the underlying racism, the frequent quotation is another sure sign of the work's significance for modern culture and politics, or even our mental mindset. It may then come as a surprise to compare Conrad's seminal text to a work which is its very opposite in terms of at least reputation and cultural presence. George MacDonald's *Lilith* is still read only by aficionados from the metaphysical fringe, readers interested in the Oxford Inklings and their predecessors or the odd fantasy fan who would like to know about the prehistory of modern phantastic literature. The two writers, furthermore, do not share many common traits – certainly not religious views or backgrounds, though one could say that both were émigré writers living and working far from the places where they grew up. MacDonald, the Scottish writer, spent much of his life in Italy, while Conrad was born in the Ukraine and sailed for some 20 years around the world before settling down in England and becoming a writer.

However, the two books I should like to compare, were written in the same last decade of the 19th century and thus may both reflect similar preoccupations and concerns belonging to fin de siècle culture. Even at a first reading, one notices that both works pay attention to similar archetypes, symbols and motifs.

Above all, both seem to paint a sinister dimension underlying the surfaces of everyday worlds. In this paper, I wish to point out to what extent these two stories overlap and where they differ. The aim of this kind of mapping is a step toward a mutual interpretation which may highlight deficiencies as well as achievement in both. What, for example, would be the implications, if we, for one moment at least, were to read Conrad's work as a spiritual quest and MacDonald's fantasy as a novel about imperialism and colonialism? Where would their common ground be found?

Joseph Conrad wrote *Heart of Darkness* between December 1898 and February 1899 and published it first in three monthly issues in *Blackwood's Magazine* in the spring of 1899. It appeared in book form three years later. The story is based on his experiences when he travelled up the Congo in 1890 doing service in a Belgian owned company (Knowles/Moore 173-176). George MacDonald's *Lilith* was first written in 1890; it underwent a number of revisions and a second extended and altered version was published in 1895. Of this final work, there are four complete drafts. Justifiably, Richard Reis assumes that "the author cared very much about the work; and I am inclined to believe Greville MacDonald's assertion that his father felt it to be divinely inspired and took his responsibility most seriously." (Reis 94)

While dates and incubation period of the two works overlap to some extent, their respective places in the authors' lives are very different. For Conrad, it was one of his early works – after the Malayan novels *Almayer's Folly* and *An Outcast of the Island* – which brought him some acclaim in the English speaking world, but for MacDonald, *Lilith* came at the end of a long writing-life. However, the period Conrad covers in his book, his trip up the Congo and his so-called command of a ship, is also near the end of a phase in a life characterized by active seamanship. He was to sail for the last time in 1892/3, on the *Torrens*, twice between Britain and Australia. These were significant journeys in terms of writing and coincided with his farewell from the sea.[xi] To some extent then, the African journey anticipates the end of a lifestyle and a working habit that had been Conrad's for the last twenty years. Diseases caught on this trip, like Malaria, were to accompany him throughout his life with bouts of fever and pain. The Congo experience has also to be seen as an attempt by Conrad to find new venues in his life. However, it fitted into a certain pattern and had a deep fascination for him. As his biographer Najder writes, "Africa presented itself for want of something else. Once this possibility arose, it probably rekindled his old interest, which had been recently revived by a wave of sensational news about the African interior, connected with Henry Morton Stanley's expedition in search of Emin Pasha." (Najder 117; cf. also Youngs 182-207) In his essay, "Geography and Some Explorers", Conrad comments at length on his early interest in the blank spaces of maps as he found them in his youth. As a boy, he felt attracted to the "exciting spaces of white paper" and was quite happy that his beloved old atlas of 1852 knew nothing of the Great Lakes: "The heart of its Africa was white and big." (Conrad 1955: 13f.). When his wish came true to go there, melancholy descended on him. The other man, who had been attracted to the white heart of the continent, Stanley, had turned mystery into a "prosaic newspaper 'stunt'", while King Leopold of Belgium with other colonial powers were engaged in the "vilest scramble for loot that ever disfigured the history of human conscience and geographical exploration. What an end to the idealized realities of a boy's daydreams!" (Conrad 1955: 17)[xli]

So much for the biographical underpinning of Conrad's famous novel. It helps to see the possible functions such a story might have both for the author and his culture. Besides satisfying curiosity and a desire for adventure, there seems to be an inherently spiritual aim as well in those voyages of discovery he writes about. Not unlike a writer, the boy tries to fill up white space with his fantasies, but these are also connected to "worthy, adventurous and devoted men, nibbling at the edges, attacking from north and south and east and west, conquering a bit of truth here and a bit of truth there and sometimes swallowed up by the mystery their hearts were so persistently set on unveiling."(Conrad 1955: 13) At the end of his essay, he says about these men, discoverers and voyagers like Cook or Franklin, that they bore in their breast "a spark of the sacred fire." (Conrad 1955: 21) This is the very image which is questioned, if not ridiculed in *Heart of Darkness* where those lightbearers of European civilisation represent a regime of terrorism and exploitation hitherto unheard of. The colonial world in *Heart of Darkness* can thus be seen as the residue of a great project labelled universal enlightenment which is carried out by its European inventors. The labels work as long as one closes one's eyes before the real situation. Marlow, as Conrad's alter ego, finds himself not only on a professional commission, that is, to locate and relieve the sick Head of the Inner Station, Kurtz, but also on a personal quest which turns out to be the ultimate test to beloved notions of self and civilisation.

While Marlow's journey leads him into the deep South, Mr Vane's journey in *Lilith* goes westward. Mr. Vane's experiences with the other world and the beyond begin at a point in his life which is as critical as was Conrad's when he went to the Congo. The young bachelor has just graduated from Oxford and spends a lot of time in the library of his ancestors in a mansion. He is at a biographical crossroads and desperately needs a challenge in the real world in order to develop morally or rather, spiritually. This mission partakes of the author's mission to write this book. As MacDonald's son Greville wrote about the first draft of *Lilith*: "He was possessed by a feeling [...] that it was a mandate direct from God, for which he himself was to find form and clothing." (MacDonald 1924: 548). Though the story is devised as a personal quest, with its protagonist undergoing changes and receiving insight, it is also a story with deep implications about the social self, society and the question of greed and power over others – in other words, about issues closely linked to the age of late Victorianism and its private and colonial economy. My contention is that while MacDonald addresses these questions rather from the inside of the psyche, Conrad illuminates a moral change overcoming the individual from the outside, from actual social and geographical experience. Yet both stories converge on several levels: the dual world structure, the sense of an inverted quest in an age which has made the quest difficult, if not impossible, and above all, values. For both authors, the central question remains as to how the immaterial survives in the material world, or rather the spirit in a world more and more ruled by dehumanised forces.

Two Worlds

Both books suggest a dual world structure from the outset: there is a here and a beyond and these two territories are divided by more or less obscure demarcations, which at times can become dangerous and well-defined. Conrad's Marlow tells his company on board the *Nelly* how he got attracted to the blank spaces in Africa. They are first of all products of the imagination fired by books, pictures and commercial symbols, which, however, have a sacred undertext. Africa is embodied in a river that looks very much like the serpent in the garden of Eden: " But there was in it one river especially, a mighty big river that you could see on the map, resembling an immense snake uncoiled with its tail lost in the depths of the land. As I looked at the map of it in a shop-window it fascinated me as a snake would a bird – a silly little bird." (*Heart* 12)[xlii] The world of temptation and knowledge is still hidden behind a window. Marlow in a sense crosses the window as Vane (and Carroll's Alice) would cross mirrors when he remembers "there was a big concern, a Company for trade on that river" (*Heart* 12). He eventually presents himself to his employers in a Continental city, which is modelled on Brussels and turns out to be the gate to the otherworld. Marlow compares it to "a whited sepulchre" (*Heart* 13). He encounters two women knitting black wool who seem to be "guarding the door of Darkness" (*Heart* 14). Altogether a sense of doom and even conspiracy is to be felt. It is reinforced by his meeting with another gatekeeper, the doctor who examines his skull, probably a phrenologist. At this point we begin to surmise that the borderline between this and the other world is identical with the line dividing the outer from the inner world. The doctor - in whom one could see references to Conrad's uncle Tadeusz Bobrowski as well as to his uncle's acquaintance, a scientific collector of skulls – takes on the role of Mr. Raven in *Lilith* by making terse philosophical comments, by giving advice and by posing riddles. In this sense, both are guardians of the threshold where the traveller has to be stripped of all mental and physical baggage. As Marlow's doctor puts it: "'I always ask leave, in the interests of science, to measure the crania of those going out there,' he said. 'And when they come back too?' I asked. 'Oh, I never see them,' he remarked, 'and, moreover, the changes take place inside, you know.'" (*Heart* 15)

With this remark, the doctor somewhat maps the type of journey undertaken in Conrad's book, it is a journey that leads through the outside, the material-colonial world to the inside, which is the heart of darkness. To Marlow, as the hidden narrator says, "the meaning of an episode was not inside like a kernel, but outside, enveloping the tale which brought it out only as a glow brings out a haze." (*Heart* 9) It is also part of Conrad's narrative strategy that he very often presents surfaces which later on are decoded in their true meaning, a process known as "delayed decoding" in Conrad studies. (Watt 1980). Marlow is offended when the doctor asks him about madness in his family. He asks the doctor whether he is an "alienist" and this question entails an inkling about the alien world he is about to enter. Though Africa and the colonies seem to be on the periphery of the civilised world, he has a feeling that he is not going to another continent but to "the centre of the earth" (*Heart* 16). Marlow's journey, here reminiscent of Jules Verne's famous journey, is inscribed into a religious and mythical tradition of going to the centre as part of an initiation or a shamanistic ritual (cf. Eliade 1952: 33-72). It is an alchemical journey which is meant to bring about some kind of transformation, as the doctor indicates. But what kind of alchemy will it be?

MacDonald's *Lilith* draws similar boundaries between this and the other world, but they are much less definable or controllable. Vane like Marlow looks into a glass and is likewise hypnotized by the things he sees inside it. Interestingly, the question arises whether the mirror is a picture or what kind of medium it actually is. The same ambivalent nature could be ascribed to the shop window in Conrad. The self looking at this kind of mirror-picture will discover itself but dissolved in something else – in the one case a snake, in the other a landscape with a raven. Both situations suggest a first step of transformation taking place even before the actual journey is begun. It is an invisible, inner change that has come over the subjects.

The first thing Vane notices in the world of the picture he has entered is that his "search was vain" – certainly a pun since himself is what he must be seeking for in a looking-glass. But the world in the mirror is not the self, not as Vane knows himself, but dissolves into a system of obstacles which we call objective reality, something that keeps resisting and withstanding our ego. Reality itself begins to melt and blend, things having an "uncertain identity at the heart of them" and none of "the communicating media of this world" is fit to convey this wavering phenomenon. The loss of his old self Vane experiences as potential madness: "I looked about me, but saw no human shape. The terror that madness might be at hand laid hold upon me: must I hence forth [sic] place no confidence either in my senses or my consciousness?" (*Lilith* 9)

The raven who becomes Mr. Raven is a master of riddles and introduces Vane to the paradox of identity. It is in these philosophical disquisitions that MacDonald is much closer to Conrad's scepticism and agnosticism than to his own Christian outlook. Or, to put it differently, he develops at this point a kind of Christian existentialism, clearly ahead of his time, an idea of Christianity which encompasses psychoanalysis. While Marlow's quest is also about his own identity vis-à-vis primeval and savage urges, Vane has to come to terms with *koans* (riddles) such as this: "If you are yourself, you know that you are not somebody else; but do you know that you are yourself? Are you sure you are not your own father?" (*Lilith* 11) Vane, completely nonplussed, starts to forget about himself beginning with his name. The name he has received in the first world is of no interest in the second. The raven then teaches him the (post)modern lesson that identity is difference, or rather transformation:

> "Look at me," he said, "and tell me who I am."
> As he spoke, he turned his back, and instantly I knew him. He was no longer a raven, but a man above the middle height with a stoop, very thin and wearing a long black tail-coat. Again he turned and I saw him a raven." (*Lilith* 11)

Name and object switch states much like in *Alice in Wonderland*. Interestingly, Marlow's "alienist" is rather similar in appearance: "He was an unshaven little man in a thread-bare coat like a gabardine with his feet in slippers." (*Heart* 15). Wielding his callipers to measure the cranium he might look like a bird opening its beak. His advice to Marlow is not as philosophically precise or challenging as that of the raven, but it suggests a profound disturbance of the real, which comes across as allusion, insinuation and the dots of incomplete speech:

> "Pardon my questions, but you are the first Englishman coming under my observation...' I hastened to assure him I was not in the least typical. 'If I were,' said I, 'I wouldn't be talking like this with you.' 'What you say is rather profound and probably erroneous,' he said with a laugh. 'Avoid irritation more than exposure to the sun. Adieu. How do you English say, eh? Good-bye. Adieu. In the tropics one must before everything keep calm.'... He lifted a warning forefinger... '*Du calme, du calme. Adieu.*' (H 15)

Quest

Though *Heart of Darkness* is mostly seen in the context of political and psychological issues, in which colonialism and racism are of supreme importance, it is also about the definition of self versus others and thus raises psychological, moral and spiritual questions. In a sense, the book can be seen as the caricature of a sacred text, or a perverted pilgrimage. It is no coincidence that echoes of Dante's *Divine Comedy* can be found in Conrad as in MacDonald. The most explicit appears when Marlow is for the first time confronted with the terrible exploitation of Africans and the devastation wrought upon the environment. He is shocked by the waste (of drainage pipes) near the settlement and comes across a "vast artificial hole" which he tries to avoid. He enters the shade to protect himself from too much exposure to the sun, "but no sooner within than it seemed to me I had stepped into the gloomy circle of some Inferno." (*Heart* 20) While the house in Brussels has been likened to the inmost core of hell, Kurtz has been seen as a satanic figure. Critics have also suggested that Conrad like T.S. Eliot may have modified and inverted the Dantean scheme, in which, for example, the Intended is a kind of reversed Beatrice (Knowles/Moore 95-6). T.S. Eliot himself was to draw attention to the metaphysical qualities of *Heart of Darkness* when he used the famous quote "Mistah Kurtz – he dead" for his poem "The Hollow Men". Whatever the precise Dantean references and inferences, the world depicted in *Heart of Darkness* is a comment on lost or rather destroyed spirituality. Conrad points to this background by stressing sacred symbolism gone astray. From the start, Marlow has a sense that he is on an important mission, or does he? He feels rather imposed upon by the elevated pseudo-spiritual language of the woman who got him the Congo job. It reeks with ideology but uses rhetoric of the sacred:

> It appears however I was also one of the Workers, with a capital – you know. Something like an emissary of light, something like a lower sort of apostle. There had been a lot of such rot let loose in print and talk about that time, and the excellent woman living right in the rush of all that humbug got carried off her feet. She talked about the 'weaning those ignorant millions from their horrid ways,' till, upon my word, she made me quite uncomfortable. I ventured to hint that the Company was run for profit. (*Heart* 15f.)

Later on, the word "emissary" is used by the brickmaker to describe Kurtz as "an emissary of pity, and science, and progress, and devil knows what else." (*Heart* 28). In terms of sequence, this is a statement similar to the previous dialogue. An idealistic image is construed and then deflated – from "pity" a line of words descends in terms of sacred values and finally leads to the "devil". It is a type of 'delayed decoding'. Even the quest itself is something that will be understood only with delay. In the Central Station Marlow encounters "white men with long staves" (*Heart* 24), suggesting pilgrims. Some paragraphs later these men "with their absurd long staves in their hands" appear to be "faithless pilgrims bewitched inside a rotten fence" and in the next sentence the long staves turn out to be very material: they are ivory tusks. The sacred has collapsed and has become simple greed. The holy quest, if there ever was one, is thus caricatured by its very opposite. Marlow's own quest, which is not meant to be a pilgrimage, however, leads him into the very heart of this perverted mystery. At the centre of Conrad's book one could make out a kind of satanic service. This is not only to be seen in the unspeakable rites in which Kurtz seems to have taken part, but also in the central text of this service, a kind of gospel written by the would-be priest Kurtz. His notorious report for the International Society for the Suppression of Savage Customs, a deeply ironical term for what Norbert Elias would call "the process of civilisation" uses highflown rhetoric. Kurtz soars in spiritual heights, as if he were preaching a sermon, and shows to what extent the whites have a historical mission to civilise the world. Reading it, Marlow tends to lose the argument but instead falls prey to the hypnotic power of words, taken on by a Miltonic Satan on his cosmic flight, while the spiritual is transformed into the material, the spirit into the body:

> From that point he soared and took me with him. The peroration was magnificent, though difficult to remember, you know. It gave me the notion of an exotic Immensity ruled by an august Benevolence. It made me tingle with enthusiasm. This was the unbounded power of eloquence – of words – of burning noble words. There were no practical hints to interrupt the magic current of phrases [...] (*Heart* 50f.)

Alas, savage customs cannot really be suppressed, as this report itself manifests. On the margins Marlow discovers "luminous and terrifying like a flash of lightning in a serene sky" those disastrous words "'Exterminate all the brutes'" (*Heart* 51). Again, a sacred surface, which had only served as a cover-up for greed, is destroyed. Thus, at the centre of Marlow's quest, the janus-face of progress lifts its head another time. Here, with Kurtz's genius as a focus, Marlow perceives both "the pulsating of light or the deceitful flow from the heart of an impenetrable darkness." (*Heart* 48) The quest for Kurtz is also a quest for the source of language and creativity, of which Marlow might be less aware than the narrator telling Marlow's story or the author himself. For at the root of this quest is something indissolubly bound up with the project of writing, of secondary creation by words. Kurtz is a most gifted creature, as we learn through various reports; he is, or was a painter, composer, journalist and all of

Europe has contributed to this Kurtz. But essentially he is a literary man, an author, someone who wields power through language. It is through his hypnotic voice that he enchants and corrupts:

> [...] of all his gifts the one that stood out pre-eminently, that carried with it a sense of real presence, was his ability to talk, his words – the gift of expression, the bewildering, the illuminating, the most exalted and the most contemptible [...] (*Heart* 48).

At this point the book becomes self-referential, a profound questioning, that is, of the nature of the writer with his gift of the gab, the one who uses words in order to manipulate people, one who is always tempted to make a good lie in order to impress or command interest. In this sense, Marlow himself learns a lesson by becoming creative at the end of his story. When he faces Kurtz's Intended in the White City, he has to produce a lie in order to save her beautiful world. This can obviously be read as a comment on a world which survives by lying. It marks the completion of an inverted quest whose aim is not truth but lies. Marlow has become the emissary of a god that has died and now reports to his priestess, thus keeping up a fake religion. Conrad has strewn the signs of this inversion of the sacred all over the text and one may go so far as to say that the book itself is structured on this inversion. *Heart of Darkness* is subversive vis-à-vis current ideologies of Empire and social respectability, a fact which does not exclude that the book may also confirm stereotypes and conventions, since Marlow is also a conventional man.[xliii]

Mr. Vane in MacDonald's *Lilith* is no less conventional and yet is sent on a quest. He is, like Marlow, a bachelor. His entry into the other world beyond the mirror is, much as Marlow's journey, characterised by disorientation, puzzlement, the necessity of redefining oneself and the possibility of destruction. Both encounter personalities whom they are unable to understand and who lead lives outside their ken; in this both travellers share Alice's experiences in Wonderland. Both journeys belong to the type of initiation rituals in which the candidate has to undergo suffering and challenge down to outright dissolution and destruction of self. They are descents into the underworld and hence follow archetypal patterns, at least up to a certain point. Vane's quest begins with the *koans* with which the Raven confronts him, riddles, that are meant to shake his fundamentals of world conception: "Where is *there*?" asks the Raven for example, and provokes Vane when he claims that he "know[s] nothing about whereness." Indeed, according to him, the universe itself "is a riddle trying to get out." (*Lilith* 45) The raven, and the alienist "measure" the neophyte before they send him into the interior, into his initiation, that is. Mr. Raven challenges not only his belief in the three dimensions by positing at least seven, but also his confidence in the Aristotelian theorem of identity. In Raven's world, "two things, or any parts of them, could occupy the same space" (*Lilith* 33); nothing is solid and things melt into other things or beings. This is a mental prelude to the events awaiting him in the country beyond the mirror and in this respect they are also questions faced by neurology and philosophy today. For example, Vane wants to know how free he is and is answered that a "man is as free as he chooses to make himself". Vane is offended: "You wrong me in the very essence of my individuality!" (*Lilith* 18) This seems to be a good summing-up of the discussions that are now raging between theology, philosophy and neurology ever since Benjamin Libet proved a certain type of determination in our acts (cf. Geyer 2004). Vane also learns about the function of names at the very moment when he has lost his (*Lilith* 11) and is taught about the workings of memory: "*There is such a thing as remembering without recognising the memory in it.*" (*Lilith* 37) Later on, when Lilith is in her final phase and is forced to give up herself - or is it her Self ?-,there is, bound up with the theological question, a very acute sense of how thought seems to be related to self, i.e. the essence of consciousness: "My own thought makes me me; my own thought of myself is me." (*Lilith* 209)

Vane's encounters with the Raven drive him to the brink of madness, a danger present in both Conrad's and MacDonald's novel. While Conrad's alienist drops some ominous words, Mr. Vane has to come to terms with the puzzling and bewildering vision of the Raven. Madness for Vane takes on an architectural space. It is symbolised in the garret above the library, "the brooding brain of the building" (*Lilith* 13), and this garret reminds him of his own brain: "'If I know nothing of my own garret,' I thought, 'what is there to secure me against my own brain? Can I tell what it is even now generating? – what thought it may present me the next moment, the next month, or a year away? What is at the heart of my brain? What is behind my *think*? Am *I* there at all? Who, what am I?'" (*Lilith* 13). His journey into the darkness of himself is also a journey into the brain of someone thinking him, as he has to learn later on. The black ellipsoid chamber in which he will meet Lilith for a second time turns out to be her brain! (*Lilith* 143). In a metaphorical sense, Marlow too finds himself inside the brain of Kurtz, whom he somehow understands more and more while at the same time rejecting him. When the crisis reaches its peak, the world outside becomes the inside and vice versa: "I confounded the beat of the drum with the beating of my heart [...]" (*Heart* 64)

For Vane, fundamental concepts such as space and time are exploded and with them identity dissolves. But this loss prepares the protagonist for the encounter with females he has never been confronted with before – the females in his soul.

Like Marlow, he is plunged into a completely alien world in which, at first sight, nothing reminds him of his past self and past or parallel environment. No more libraries or even books, no more fathers and (male) teachers – except for the raven- , no more the secluded life of a bachelor who is devoted to science and literature. Instead he is whirled from one gloomy scene into the next and yet follows a circular path pulling him again and again to a centre. In the same vein, Marlow crosses the circles of an inferno which are marked by the White City, the arrival at Boma, the coast, the Central Station and the Inner Station, where Kurtz reigns. Vane travels from the House of the Dead through barren landscapes, deserts, encounters the half-dead woman who turns out to be Lilith, and then joins up with the children to attack the city of Bulika. At the same time, these movements only count in one world, in the other one they do not take *place* in the literal sense. As Colin Manlove pointed out: "In *Lilith*, however, Vane in a sense never moves from his house: Mr Raven tells him, 'you have not yet left your house, neither has your house left you!'" (Manlove 69)

He moves in circles or rather spirals, which, in MacDonald's spatial imagination, has a sacramental meaning, reflecting the ascent or descent of the soul in the material world (cf. Manlove 1982: 70), a symbolism obviously close to Dante's *Divine Comedy* (cf. Kranz 1989). On his quest, Vane is, much like Marlow, exposed to the most dismal experiences. The worlds he passes are sloughs of Despond, they reek with death, danger, aggression and are only at times relieved by the song of happy innocent children. Wild creatures roam about, and constantly threaten the protagonist. The landscape is barren, or a dark wood, a desert and for a long while drought rains. If we were to locate the setting in real geography we would probably find it in the Middle East – the area haunted originally by Lilith – or, as I would also suggest, Africa. Fauna and flora anyway point to these areas: there are lions, flamingos, leopards, monkeys, snakes and elephants. And there are creepy beings which are beautiful as well, like those "slimy things", the water-snakes in Coleridge's *Rime of the Ancient Mariner*, e.g. the large serpent "covered from head to distant tail with feathers of glorious hues." (*Lilith* 49) Mythologically informed readers may be reminded of the feathered serpent of the Aztec god Quetzalcoatl who later turned into Venus, the morning star. MacDonald's phantastic world in its mythical dance encompassing ages and continents, however, is beyond geography. His territory is a country of the mind.

Like Marlow, Vane also encounters human-made catastrophe, a pitiful world of reckless power and greed that subjugates a whole population. Lilith's reign over Bulika is comparable to Kurtz's terror over his subjects. Both are killers and vampires of those they rule. This corresponds to the weakness attributed to a powerless people. For Vane, the children in the wood are lovely but also pitiful. In this sense, they share characteristics of the black population as seen by Marlow. The Africans have certain natural qualities which make them likeable to Marlow, but they also suffer from a lack of power and identity, nameless and speechless as they appear in his rendering. In the same manner, the children remain "frozen in childhood", as Karen Schaafsma put it (Schaafsma 56). Vane then behaves like the benevolent coloniser: "Vane appoints himself their champion, but his plan for their benefit is typically arrogant." (Schaafsma 56). His quest turns into warfare, in which he incites the children to attack Bulika, an act leading to an empty victory. At the end, he loses Lona, though he meeting her again in a dream. "Life was a cosmic holiday" (*Lilith* 255), but eventually, after the dream, he finds himself alone again in his library, discussing with himself whether it was his brain or his fever that made him dream these things. Undoubtedly, doubtlessness will come, but only in the next life (*Lilith* 264). Marlow is unable to tell the truth to the Intended and Vane just waits for another life to lose his vanity: two tales of unending quests.

Values

The major difference, as I see it, between *Heart of Darkness* and *Lilith* is to be found in the question of gender, or in the role and importance of men and women. While Vane from the male world of his father's library with its librarian and male ancestors is tumbled into an almost completely female world, the obverse seems to happen to Marlow. Marlow is sent on his quest by the help of his female relation in the White City, Marguerite Poradowska in Conrad's real life. In spite of his misogyny, it is the women who help him get the command of a ship in the Congo: "Then – would you believe it – I tried the women. I, Charlie Marlow, set the women to work – to get a job! Heavens!" (*Heart* 12) He meets the two black women and then is hurled into the inhuman world of African disaster. Women play no further role until he sees a portrait painted by Kurtz of his Intended. Kurtz and Marlow share an understanding to keep the women out and to leave them in their world of beautiful things, an exclusion of women much debated in feminist criticism (cf. Straus 2004). At a decisive moment, however, the female returns with a vengeance in Africa when, in the shape of a savage woman, she performs some kind of dance ritual. Here, the dangerous side of the female, its savage nature is stressed. This woman, with her tusks of elephants as ornamentation, is connected to the wild life of animals, to aggression and war:

> She walked with measured steps, draped in striped and fringed cloths, treading the earth proudly with a slight jingle and flash of barbarous ornaments. She carried her head high, her hair was done in the shape of a helmet, she had

> [...] a crimson spot on her tawny cheek [...] bizarre things, charms, gifts of witch-men [...] (*Heart* 60)

Her affinity with such powerful females as Rider Haggard's Ayesha or MacDonald's Lilith becomes evident. More precisely, the crimson spots on her cheek remind one of the spots ascribed to Lilith or to the spotted leopard whose form she takes from time to time. These spots may indeed carry a theological symbolism denoting sinfulness (Hein 104). In a sense, Conrad's savage woman impersonates the whole landscape and experience of the Congo:

> And in the hush that had fallen suddenly upon the whole sorrowful land, the immense wilderness, the colossal body of the fecund and mysterious life seemed to look at her, pensive, as though it had been looking at the image of its own tenebrous and passionate soul. (*Heart* 60)

It may be timely to remind ourselves of Marlow's youthful fantasies when he correlated the Congo river on the map to a snake (*Heart* 12). He is hypnotised by the snake on the map as are the observer's of the woman appearing in the wild.

This correlation of land, woman and snake is characteristic of Lilith as well and leads us to the Grail legend, symbolistic landscapes and to the Jewish folklore from which MacDonald's figure originates. In contrast to the Grail stories which are centred around a lame fisher king whose country lies waste, in *Lilith* the waste land is due to a powerful woman and to the weakness of its inhabitants. However, psychic state and country are intricately related. When Lilith finds a way back to her soul and is – like the princess in MacDonald's fairy tale "The Light Princess" – able to weep tears, the country's rivers start flowing again. Vane, then, can be seen as a kind of Parsifal who has to ask the right question, or rather who has to do the right action. Like Parsifal he cannot do it without making a number of terrible mistakes or ending up in double binds, such as the re-awakening of Lilith at the beginning of his journey (Chapter 18). Similarly, the sick Kurtz personifies the world he has created around him, while his Parsifal Marlow is equally unable to ask the right question, from which a lie results, the misleading answer to Kurtz's Intended when she asks him what Kurtz's last words were. Symbolism, as Adelheid Kegler has pointed out, provided the matrix for much of MacDonald's imagination, and, as Ian Watt has shown, this is equally true for Conrad (A. A. Kegler 2005, Watt 1980). One only has to remember the famous drawing by Conrad representing a dancing woman with a snake curled around her (reproduced in Meyer 1967: 326-27), on which the psychoanalytic critic Bernard C. Meyer has this to say: "Both his writings and his drawings are liberally sprinkled with references to birds and snakes."

(Meyer 331). For Meyer, this association is a clear sign of a more or less unconscious repulsion and attempt to reject the female sides of himself, something that is clearly related to Marlow's misogyny. Both writers certainly follow patterns of late nineteenth-century representations of women in the garb of femme fatale, the vampire, bat and serpent. To this extent, they express fear and fascination, taboo and repulsion as far as the other sex is concerned. Conrad, however, is closer to the stereotype, as for example represented by Haggard's *She* and *Ayesha*, all the more so since his women are rare in *Heart of Darkness*. Here we find an essential difference from MacDonald, whose work is filled with a number of women: Eve, Lilith, Lona, Mara and others, though they are never quite individualised since they serve allegorical functions as well. In a sense, however, MacDonald tries to tackle psychological problems Conrad at this point seems to shun by perpetuating male myths of women, which are in part about their exclusion. By taking up the legendary figure of Lilith, MacDonald entered troubled waters. In ancient Jewish legends to be found in Kabbalistic and folk lore, Lilith was Adam's first wife, who was not willing to subject herself to him. She was expelled and revenged herself by killing all males and returning as a ghost or vampire to haunt Adam's new relationship with Eve (cf. Reis 1972: 149, n.17). This figure drew a lot of interest in the late nineteenth century because for some it posited as the subversive and rebellious woman, for others as the dangerous power to be subjected by Christianity and patriarchy (cf. McGillis 1979; Harris 1986).

While the dancing woman in Conrad might be a reflection of Lilith, one could also suggest that Conrad portrayed the male equivalent of Lilith in no other than Kurtz. Kurtz has shed the trappings of so-called civilisation and exchanged them for his prehistoric self, a self that precedes his European self, in a similar way as Lilith precedes Eve. Both books stress the return to the worlds of prehistory, to the worlds before writing and cities. Marlow evokes the feelings of "wanderers on a prehistoric earth, on an earth that wore the aspect of an unknown planet. We could have fancied ourselves the first of men taking possession of an accursed inheritance [...]" (*Heart* 37). In *Lilith* there is similar sense of an early world or unknown planet on which more than one moon shines (*Lilith* 48). And as in the paradox of first men "taking possession of an accursed inheritance", even the paradisal world of Adam and Eve has a history.

Whatever the gender prejudices at work, both writers, whether Conrad in his colonial context or MacDonald in his fantastic-theological one try to seek an answer to the question why the world is fallen and why we are still falling from grace. Conrad certainly does not point to Christianity, and nor is there in MacDonald much orthodox Christianity. But both address an evil that became more and more prominent at the end of the century and was related to the immense technological progress of the age: greed and the lust for power. Kurtz and Lilith have this in common that they are unable to give up control and to share power. Even Kurtz in his younger days, when he was a shining polymath and had the making of a genius, was trying to explore the limits of power over others. Or as the Manager says after Kurtz's death: "He electrified large meetings [...] He would have been a splendid leader of an extreme party." (*Heart* 71). His voice envelops and enthrals and exerts power over people and there is an overtly oral nature to his greed:

> I saw him open his mouth wide – it gave him a weirdly voracious aspect as though he had wanted to swallow all the air, all the earth, all the men before him. (*Heart* 59)

The symbol and commodity associated with him is ivory and the greed for ivory destroys the land and the people. The same applies to the greed for gems that is found with the inhabitants of Bulika and which helps them support Lilith's reign. Interestingly, Lilith, in her confessional poem, describes how she tinted her skin "to ivory tone." (*Lilith* 153) The name of Bulika – which has been likened to Babylon through a blend of *bull* and *icon* (Reis 97; on Bulika cf. K. Kegler 1995) could also be connected to *bulimy* or 'bull-like', morbid hunger and emotional disorder, a meaning on record in English since the 17th century (OED). If one were to pursue this oral element in *Lilith* one might find that the Hebrew meaning of *Mara* is bitter and that this taste usually restrains the appetite. Another equivalent of this emotional disorder can be found in Lilith who is unable to open her hand, which will be severed ultimately – a grotesque and inverted parallel to those severed hands the Belgian colonisers expected to see as a token for Africans who were killed because they had not delivered enough ivory or rubber (Hochschild 164-66).

In light of the oral imagery in both novels, one can see to what extent they attempt to cope with the psychological and social dynamics of greed. In Conrad's case, there is exploration of this sin on various levels: political and individual, but he also indicates religious views, as we have seen. Specifically greed might be in focus, when Conrad's narrator describes Marlow in a particular posture: "he had the pose of a Buddha preaching in European clothes and without a lotus-flower" (*Heart* 10, also 76). The basic teaching of Buddhism is, as Conrad's readers might have been aware of, that desires are the root of all evil and suffering. But this teaching takes place without the lotus-flower, that is, without the Asian background. The teaching rather adopts a European garment: European words, values, experiences, to which also the death of god belongs, atheism, scepticism, even cynicism and the loss of truth. MacDonald uses a story and dialogues steeped in theological and metaphysical patterns, but are they Christian? Is his dream-world governed by a Christian or

Jewish God? I think there are only hints of this religion and MacDonald is on the way to something new. Part of it is the feminist message that men have to come to terms with women and the female inside them; part of it is also that greed turns any Eden into nightmare, and there is very little left of Eden though we are meant to meet with Adam and Eve. It is a world where death reigns and desire, a deeply confusing world produced by brains and libraries, the horrors of theology and metaphysics. However, in spite of H.G. Wells' comparing MacDonald's imagination to the many-breasted Diana of Ephesus, "an image that is depraved to the hieroglyphic level" (Wells 13), there are glimpses of new dimensions and new concepts of the human. As opposed to Marlow's 'Buddhism', MacDonald integrates evolutionary thought in his theology. There is, according to the Raven, a beast-self, a bird-self, a tree-self and even a crystal-self within each of us, "and I don't know how many more" (*Lilith* 28). MacDonald soars into the heights of potentiality reminiscent of Socialist utopian philosophies such as Ernst Bloch's when he says:

> I saw now that a man alone is but a being that may become a man – that he is but a need, and therefore a possibility […] Only by the reflex of other lives can he ripen his specialty, develop the idea of himself […] I, poorest of creatures, was yet a possible man! (*Lilith* 105)

Lilith, as Roderick McGillis once put it succinctly, "is the woman who refuses to be written." (McGillis 1990 51), and similarly, Kurtz is the man who refuses to be expressed. One of the reasons is that those who are trying to express them are still in a state of possibility. As they do not know who they are themselves, it is nearly impossible for both Vane nor Marlow to come to terms with the powerful beings they are confronted with and which reflect parts of themselves, their terrifying potentialities. In this sense, both novels are ways of writing about this impossibility and of expressing that which refuses to be written.

Works Cited

Conrad, Joseph. *Heart of Darkness*. Ed. by Robert Kimbrough. New York: Norton Critical Edition 1988.

—. "Geography and Some Explorers" . In *Last Essays*. London: Dent 1955. 1-21.

Eliade, Mircea. *Images et symbols. Essais sur le symbolisme magico-religieux*. Paris: Gallimard 1952.

Farn, Regelind. *Colonial and Postcolonial Rewritings of "Heart of Darkness". A Century of Dialogue with Joseph Conrad*. Boca Raton, Florida: dissertation.com 2005.

Geyer, Christian, ed. *Hirnforschung und Willensfreiheit. Zur Deutung der neuesten Experimente*. Frankfurt/M.: Suhrkamp 2004.

Harris, Elree Irene. "The Wounded Angel": The Lilith Myth in Nineteenth and Twentieth- Century British Literature. PhD, University of Utah 1986. DAI 47 (No. 08), February 1987 3047A.

Hein, Rolland. *The Harmony Within. The Spiritual Vision of George MacDonald*. Grand Rapids, Michigan: Christian UP 1982.

Hochschild, Adam. *King Leopold's Ghost. A Story of Greed, Terror, and Heroism in Colonial Africa*. New York: Houghton Mifflin 1998.

Kegler, Adelheid. "Drunten in der Tiefe: Die Symbolistische Landschaft George MacDonald." *Inklings Jahrbuch* 23 (2005), 10-31.

Kegler, Karl. " Eine Stadt aus Kristall. Sodom – Bulika – Jerusalem." *Inklings Jahrbuch* 13 (1995), 75-89.

Knowles, Owen and Gene Moore, eds. *Oxford Reader's Companion to Conrad*. Oxford: Oxford UP 2000.

Kranz, Gisbert, "Dante im Werk von George MacDonald". *Deutsches Dante Jahrbuch* Band 64, 1989, 41-60.

MacDonald, George. *Lilith. A Romance*. Whitethorn, CA: Johannesen Printing 1994.

MacDonald, Greville. *George MacDonald and His Wife*. London: George Allen & Unwin 1924.

McGillis, Roderick F. "George MacDonald and the Lilith Legend in the XIXth Century." *Mythlore* 6 (Winter 1979), 3-11.

McGillis, Roderick F. "Phantastes and Lilith: Femininity and Freedom", in William Raeper, ed., *The Gold Thread, Essays on George MacDonald*, Edinburgh UP 1990.31- 55.

Manlove, Colin. "The Circle of the Imagination: George MacDonald's *Phantastes* and *Lilith*." *Studies in Scottish Literature* vol. XVII (1982), 55-80.

Meyer, Bernard C. *Joseph Conrad. A Psychoanalytic Biography*. Princeton, NJ: Princeton UP 1967.

Najder, Zdzisław. *Joseph Conrad. A Chronicle*. Cambridge: Cambridge UP 1983.

Reis, Richard. *George MacDonald's Fiction*. Eureka, CA: Sunrise Books 1989.

Schaafsma, Karen. "The Demon Lover – Lilith and the Hero in Modern Literature." *Extrapolations* 28 (1987), 52-61.

Straus, Nina Pelikan. "The Exclusion of the Intended from Secret Sharing in Conrad's *Heart of Darkness*, in Moore, Gene, ed. *Joseph Conrad's* Heart of Darkness. *A Casebook*. Oxford: Oxford UP 2004, 197-218.

Watt, Ian. *Conrad in the Nineteenth Century*. London: Chatto & Windus 1980.

Wells, Herbert George. "On George MacDonald." *Saturday Review* 80, 19 October 1895, 513. Reprinted in Patrick Parrinder, Robert M. Philmus, eds. *H.G. Wells – Literary Criticism*. Brighton: Harvester Press 1980.

Youngs, Tim. *Travellers in Africa. British Travelogues, 1850-1900*. Manchester: Manchester UP 1994.

Zhuwarara, Rino. "*Heart of Darkness* Revisited." In Gene M. Moore, ed. *Joseph Conrad's* Heart of Darkness. *A Casebook*. Oxford: Oxford UP 2004, 219-242.

[xxxix] Reginald Farn (2006) analyses some 30 novels/travelogues using Conrad's work as a basis; one could easily add a dozen more.

[xl] On one of these crossings a sick Cambridge student became the first reader of his first novel and decided about Conrad's future as a writer when he expressed his interest in it. On another crossing, Conrad got to know two passengers returning from a quest for R.L. Stevenson in the Pacific, E.R. Sanderson and John Galsworthy, who both became important as friends and literary advisers. Cf. Najder 153-157.

[xli] Conrad does not mention these names but they are certainly meant here.

[xlii] *Heart* henceforth refers to *Heart of Darkness* (Conrad 1988).

[xliii] Cf. the debate surrounding Chinua Achebe's famous indictment suggesting that Conrad was a racist. Cf. the articles by Achebe and others in the Norton Critical Edition of *Heart of Darkness* (Conrad 1988. 251-285) and Zhuwarara 2004.

Chapter Nine

Liminality as Psychic Stage in MacDonald's *Lilith*

Roderick McGillis

"we breathed homeward our longing desires"
(*Lilith* Chapter XLV)

Robert Collins begins his exploration of liminality in *Lilith* (1994) by examining a passage from the book's penultimate chapter. I'll begin my exploration in the book's second chapter, "The Mirror." In this chapter, Vane follows a shadowy figure to regions of his house he had never before known, and in a small chamber in the expansive garret he comes across "a tall mirror with a dusty face, old fashioned and rather narrow – in appearance an ordinary glass" (*Lilith* 7). The glass, however, proves to be anything but "ordinary." Like mirrors in many of MacDonald's books, this one proves to be a portal, a threshold, a doorway, an entrance to another world from the one in which the protagonist lives in what we might, loosely, think of as normal reality. The reality beyond the portal, inside or on the other side of the mirror, differs from the reality we experience in the here and now. And so we have at least two realities, one on either side of the mirror. What are these realities? Or more precisely, what function does the mirror serve in the negotiation between these realities? If liminality is relevant to MacDonald's vision, then the mirror itself is a liminal zone, a place where one passes between realities; the mirror activates a rite of passage. In this function of passageway, the mirror is similar to the many doors that Collins cites in *Lilith*: coffin lids, a masked door, a closet door, books, graves, and even a fountain (*Lilith* 3, 2). Each of these portals indicates the intensely inward movement of this book. The rite of passage enacts a psychic change, usually the change from immaturity to maturity. In Freudian terms, what we have is the individual's encounter with forces (usually manifested in the father) demanding repression, demanding the individual turn from libidinal obsessions to socially sanctioned actions. MacDonald's emphasis on the Library as the location for Vane's experiences (he begins and ends in the library of his house), and Vane's description of his own "mental peculiarities" (*Lilith* 1) cue the reader to the psychological interest the story takes in its protagonist. *Lilith* is the story of Vane's passage from one state of psychic development to another. His story is the story of the transition from adolescence to adulthood, that transition that MacDonald chronicles many times in his works, perhaps most directly in his essay, "A Sketch of Individual Development" (1882).

The mirror has a rich history as a trope, both as a dark glass hiding from us the vision of truth and spiritual finality and as a luminous surface that reflects truth and wonderment (see LaBossiere and Schell). The mirror has also served as a metaphor for the book itself when writers spoke of holding a mirror up to nature (see Abrams). The mirror has been the soul, the conscience, and the window to all things essential. The mirror has also had its narcissistic implications. For Jacques Lacan, the mirror usefully images the transition from an oceanic jouissance into desire, and I think Lacan's insight might be helpful for our understanding of *Lilith*. If Vane carries any message back to us at the end of the book when he fails to find fulfillment and a place in the "city among the blue clouds" (*Lilith* 259), then this message has something to do with patience. Collins, like a number of readers, finds the ending of *Lilith* disconcertingly abstruse or at least not completely satisfying (see Wolff 365-371, Robb 107, for example). He senses an "air of didactic failure" at the end, although he suggests that the failure "is perhaps as likely to be that of [the book's] readers as of its author" (Collins 5). I like this. I think we are wise to defer to an author, even in these heady days of perplexity at the notion of authorship itself. MacDonald found inspiration for *Lilith* in several places, not least in the work of William Blake, and like Blake, he had a vision that contemplated both the possibility of completeness and the acceptance of incompleteness. Things will be complete, but not in our knowing this side of the grave. *Lilith* is, as Manlove says, eschatology (Manlove 92), but eschatology only contemplates an end, it cannot accomplish it. MacDonald returns again and again to the notion of "endless ending"; things do end, but we can only speculate and imagine an ending. We cannot experience ending, that is an apocalyptic ending, not yet, not until, perhaps, our life becomes that dream that both Vane and Novalis mention. While we exist this side of perfection, we can only see what the eye/I offers, what Vane identifies, when he looks at Eve for the first time, as "continuous creation" (*Lilith* 26).

Myths, of course, imagine both beginnings and endings. They are ways we have of speculating on the why of things, and in speculating, myths offer not explanations in any absolute sense, but rather comfort, what Tolkien called "consolation" (Tolkien 60). The consolation is for the condition in which we find ourselves, a condition that is perpetually between, perpetually longing for completion, perpetually aware of completion's inevitability, and also of completion's unknowability. We know and yet we do not know. We see by glimpses only. The dream continues, even while we wait for the dream to become reality. MacDonald's prose delivers paradox as one of its most insistent rhetorical devices, and it does so precisely to communicate this condition of knowing and not knowing. Perhaps this is the condition of myth itself. Certainly, we might argue that this is the condition of human material existence as it tries to understand itself in non-material ways. Myth is one attempt we make to understand that which exceeds material knowing, but myth itself derives not from some metaphysical zone, but from the very materiality we sense is only part of our experience.

Another way of articulating this sense of our being "in between" is for me to contemplate the conception of "home." As Collins points out, *Lilith* offers speculation on home as "the only place where you can go out and into . . . the one place, if you do but find it, where you may go out and in both, is home" (Collins 4; *Lilith* 12). The Raven tells Vane: "Home is ever so far away in the palm of your hand, and how to get there it is of no use to tell you" (*Lilith* 45). Home is, in other words, Reality, that condition in which we are at one with things. In Lacanian terms, Home is that amorphous and chaotic state of being in which subject and object are one. Home is where we come from and where we hope to return. It is the Imperial Palace from which we come and the Celestial City to which we hope to go. To be home is to be prior to birth. To be home is to be dead. Reality lies prior to being in the world and beyond the grave. From a psychoanalytic perspective, Home is where desire finds completion, and when we reflect that desire can, by definition, not find completion in consciousness we realize just how elusive Home is; from a spiritual perspective, Home is in the ether, in the Celestial City, the city in the clouds from which Vane is turned away. *Lilith* emphasizes the attractions and the elusiveness of Home partly through MacDonald's language that is necessarily paradoxical. Our life is no dream, and yet it ought to become one; our life in the mundane world is a dream from which we will awake to find ourselves in Reality. As Stephen Prickett puts it, at the end of *Lilith* "It is not clear if [Vane] has at last 'awoken' from death in that other world, only to be returned to this, or if he has merely dreamed that he has awoken—so that his existence in this world is only part of the dream until he finally 'awakes' " (192). The point is that humans, like Mr. Vane, yearn for Home, but fear it at the same time because Home contains death as well as life. When Eve enters the cemetery, Vane finds her as lovely as "Beatrice in the white rose of the redeemed" (30), but when Adam invites him to sleep in the cemetery, Vane refuses. He is not yet ready to "come alive and die" (34).

Vane's experience nicely corresponds to Lacan's Mirror Stage (*Ecrits* 1-7). Clearly, Vane is at a transitional stage in his life, having recently completed his studies at Oxford. His parents are no longer living, and he will shortly assume "the management of the estate" (1). Commentators on *Lilith* sometimes see the plot as chronicling Vane's search for his father, and to a certain extent, this is the case (see Wolf 331; Hein 404, although Hein's "the Father and the Son" differ from Wolff's father). His reading of his father's manuscript starts him on his journey in earnest. But we can, I think, assume that both parents are important for Vane, the mother representing that Home Vane desires and the father representing duty and labor associated with what Lacan terms the Symbolic. I might as well come clean and state that I am using Lacan's three "stages" (the Real, the Imaginary, and the Symbolic) to structure my thinking about *Lilith* here. The Real I am considering as Home. We might think of the Real in a Platonic sense as an Ideal, and this would not be completely askew; however, Lacan's Real is a psychic phenomenon rather than an ideational or spiritual one. It exists at all times as the "place" and the "time" we yearn to return to, and as in Freud it has connections with the Mother. Vane's desire for a variety of female figures – Eve, Mara, Lilith, and Lona – expresses his desire for the lost mother. These women have no existence outside of Vane's desire; they are symptoms of his desire. In other words, the entire story constitutes Vane's fantasy. We may remember Lacan's infamous assertion that woman does not exist (*Feminine Sexuality* 145). The non-existence of woman is especially clear in the case of Lilith herself. Vane brings her to life when he cares for her beside the stream in Chapters XVIII and XIX, and later in Chapter XXIX Adam reads a poem in which we learn that in the earlier incident Lilith took shape from Vane's own desire. The poem's speaker is Lilith:

> For by his side, I lay, a bodiless thing;
> I breathed not, saw not, felt not, only thought,
> And made him love me—with a hungering
> After he knew not what—if it was aught
> Or but a nameless something that was wrought
> By him out of himself . . .
> (150)

Lilith clothes herself, she says, "in the likeness true/Of that idea where his soul did cleave" (151). Before Vane gives Lilith life, she is "bodiless," a negation, virtually a nothingness. Clearly, from one perspective Lilith represents the ontological certainty of evil, but from another perspective, she represents only possibility and desire, nothing more and nothing less. We might remember that she has little or no power of agency in herself; she needs Vane and we can assume that she also needs the Great Shadow that appears to control her. In other words, Lilith is a creature of male desire. She exists as evidence of the male fantasy of fullness. She is, strangely, Vane's *objet a*, that thing that activates and focuses his desire for the Real. Insofar as she is unattainable, she is the Real. She represents indulgence, hedonism, algolagnia, chaos, darkness drawing down, and ecstasy. We can assume that she will be waiting for him, along with Lona and the others, when he eventually dies into life.

Vane comes to Lilith after looking in and passing through a mirror. The mirror stage in Lacan is the moment of separation, the moment in which the subject (in this case Vane) becomes aware of otherness. What the infant sees in the mirror is a reflection of himself; Vane sees not himself when he looks in the mirror, but what he does see is an aspect of himself, his psychic geography, as it were. Manlove comments that "all the figures in *Lilith* are, as it were, parts of one huge imagination" (90). Indeed, everything in *Lilith* is part of Vane's (and by extension, MacDonald's) imagination. Once on the other side of the mirror, Vane discovers that he has an identity problem, he understands that "I did not know myself" (11). Later, when he succors Lilith, he learns for the first time "what solitude meant." He tell us: "I saw now that a man alone is but a being that may become a man—that he is but a need, and therefore a possibility." The perfection of man depends upon otherness. Vane asserts:

> A man to be perfect—complete, that is, in having reached the spiritual condition of persistent and universal growth, which is the mode wherein he inherits the infinitude of his Father—must have the education of a world of fellow-men.
> (105)

He uses the word "gaze" to indicate his specular relationship to the woman he is nurturing, and this fits with the Lacanian notion of the gaze as the subject's construction of the Imaginary "other" that derives from the reflected self first perceived in the mirror. To put this bluntly, I note that when Vane brings Lilith back to life, he is creating his Imaginary, that ideal self he would like to enjoy. The creation or even the awareness of the Imaginary precipitates the subject into the Symbolic, the world most of us inhabit, the world of language and quotidian reality, what Lacan refers to as the "law of the Father." This is the world that Lilith also inhabits, a world of getting and spending, in which possession is the most prized condition. This is the world in which self and other confront each other and communicate with language, in one sense or another.

Collins notes that in the world behind the mirror, Vane encounters difficulty with language. He puts it this way: "the most critical incompatibility Vane discovers concerns Language" (2). In Lacan's view, language and the unconscious share a structure. Like aspects of the unconscious, language is arbitrary. Lacan here picks up on Saussurian linguistics, the notion that the relationship between a word and that which it signifies is agreed upon uneasily in that word and signification are more often than not elusive, and they are certainly arbitrary. Words are "live things" that scurry from person to person and from meaning to meaning. Vane tells us more than once that he has difficulty matching word and meaning, and the reason for this is simply that words are incompetent to say anything with finality or complete accuracy. At one point, he interrupts the narrative to explain that he is engaged in a "constant struggle to say what cannot be said with even an approach to precision." He notes that where he is a "single thing would sometimes seem to be and mean many things" (46). MacDonald is here echoing the Romantic idea of what Wordsworth refers to as the "sad incompetence of human speech." But this idea has relevance for the Lacanian notion of language as itself an *objet a*, that which focuses our longing, that which attempts to fill in for the absent home. Language is symbolic precisely because it is always just a cover for that which cannot be said or that which is missing. In other words, language reminds us that we lack the completeness of the Real. Once we re-enter the Real, subject and object, word and meaning will coalesce. We have a glimpse of this in Chapter XLV, "The Journey Home." Vane tell us that the "world and my being, its life and mine, were one" (255). He, Lona, and the Little Ones are on their way "home to the Father!" (255). We know what he means, but perhaps I can take the liberty of inserting a psychoanalytic observation here and point out that the "Father" inevitably represents the world separate from the Mother, and therefore we can know that Vane must find not completion, but incompletion in his journey. The law of the father dictates that the world this side of death is incomplete; it is as much a vale of longing as it is a vale of tears. Until he is truly dead, Vane can only wait, asleep or awake, wait for the end that we cannot know beyond imaginative projection.

And so we return to the end, to that point in the book when the narrative closes. Collins, like readers before him, finds the close of the book teasingly difficult. Why, he asks, does the close of the book have a "negative pattern of reversal twice repeated within a few pages" (4)? Isn't the protagonist supposed to learn something during the course of his experiences, and is not the learning process supposed to fit into a mythopoeic pattern? His sense of mythopoesis derives from C. S. Lewis's influential argument that MacDonald excels not as a literary writer, but as a myth-maker (14). For Lewis, myth appears to communicate "the quality of the real universe, the divine, magical, terrifying and ecstatic reality in which we all live" (21). Myth has a spiritual significance; without myth, life is dark and mechanical. I am not sure, however, that we need to think of myth precisely in this way. Obviously, we do have myths that contain spiritual significance, that give us glimpses of our origin and perhaps glimpses of our destination. Such myths purport to organize and even explain deep truths, to put into words that which lies deeper than words. The origins of such myths are obscure, perhaps even beyond human knowing. On the other hand, myths derive from the human imagination and when we think of myths as having their origin in human materiality, we can think of them as deliberately concerned with the stubborn facts of human interaction that involve such things as desire and relationships. If the end of *Lilith* poses a problem, then the problem may have something to do with how we interpret "myth."

One possible answer to what Collins perceives to be a problem at the book's closing lies in the notion of liminality. Perhaps the book chronicles a space between one condition and the other, between material reality and spiritual reality. But we know that MacDonald thought of these realities as "mingling" and therefore as really one reality. And Collins closes his own suggestive exploration of *Lilith* by asking "what is the significance of the 'endless ending'?" The ending of the book, he asserts, "does not seem to most serious readers to mirror what they already know of MacDonald's religious beliefs" (5). Frankly, I don't know whether I count as one of MacDonald's "serious readers," but I have never found the end of this book either a failure or negative. On the contrary, I have always found the book, ending and all, as a visionary experience that confidently speaks of human possibility even while it speaks from within an incomplete world. The myth MacDonald delivers is the myth of human possibility that includes the possibility both of victory and of failure. Victory must confront us as a possibility, as it does Vane when he approaches the City in the blue clouds, but failure is our necessary ground. Failure is necessary because without it we would have nowhere to go. Without contraries is no progression. Opposition is true friendship. Such aphorisms contain the myth I sense in *Lilith*. Vane's rite of passage takes him from a condition of relative infancy into the Symbolic. His triumph is that in passing into the Symbolic, he has learned something. He has learned of loss and its relation to desire, and he has learned patience, the patience to know that desire can only find fulfillment elsewhere, in the Real from which we are barred until death do us bring together.

The end returns us to the mother, as if Vane understands that the Real entails a necessary return of the world to the mother. He writes: "But when I wake at last into that life which, as a mother her child, carries this life in its bosom, I shall know that I wake, and shall doubt no more" (264). The symptom of Vane's longing is the series of women he meets beyond the mirror, and each of these women is, in one way or another, a mother. Child mother (Lona), demon mother (Lilith), sorrowful mother (Mara), first mother (Eve)--Vane finds each of these women attractive and compelling. And none of them can he have, at least not yet, not in the here and now of this mundane world of just three dimensions. Even seven dimensions are insufficient for *jouissance*. For now, he has the knowledge of desire's reach. Just as Lilith herself learns to relinquish false desire, the paternal desire for ownership, control, and power, so too does Vane learn the vanity of such desire. His name offers a clue. The vanity he learns to set aside is only one aspect of his name's signification; "vane" also is that which changes as the wind blows. Persistent growth is necessary to all creatures, as we see in the story of Lord and Lady Cokayne. These two grotesque and comic figures remind us of the necessary continuation of growth. "Vane" is also a variant of the older word "fane," which is a temple or church. The body as a temple dates back a long way. The bodies of Lord and Lady Cokayne are ruined temples, but reconstruction will take place, in time. My point is that Mr. Vane is changeable, he is vain, and he is also holy. He is, in short, a walking contradiction. Mr. Vane is just like the rest of us. This is why he ends up back in the library. We leave him surrounded by ghosts of possible relationship and love. The books in the Library, like the book *Lilith*, are necessary reminders of the ongoing work of understanding and connectedness.

Works Cited

Abrams, Myer H. Abrams, Myer H. *The Mirror and the Lamp*. New York: W. W. Norton, 1953.

Collins, Robert. "Liminality in MacDonald's *Lilith*." March 14, 2004. http://www.english.fau.edu/faculty/collins/lilith.htm

Hein, Rolland. *George MacDonald: Victorian Mythmaker*. Nashville, TN: Star Song, 1993.

La Bossiere, Camille and Richard Schell. "Glass, Mirror." *A Dictionary of Biblical Tradition in English Literature*. Gen. Editor, David Lyle Jeffrey. Grand Rapids, MI: William B. Eerdmans, 1992. 308-310.

Lacan, Jacques. *Ecrits*: A Selection. Trans. Alan Sheridan. New York: W. W. Norton, 1977.

Lewis, C. S. *George MacDonald: An Anthology*. London: Geoffrey Bles, 1946.

MacDonald, George. *Lilith*. Whitethorn, CA: Johannesen, 1994 (1895).

—. "A Sketch of Individual Development." *A Dish of Orts*. London: Sampson Low, Marston, 1895 (1882). 43-76.

Manlove, Colin. *The Impulse of Fantasy Literature*. Kent, OH: Kent State University P, 1983.

Mitchell, Juliet and Jacqueline Rose, eds. *Feminine Sexuality: Jacques Lacan and the ecole freudienne*. Trans. Jacqueline Rose. New York: W. W. Norton, 1985.

Prickett, Stephen. *Victorian Fantasy*. Bloomington and London: Indiana University P, 1979.

Robb. David. *George MacDonald*. Edinburgh: Scottish Academic Press, 1987.

Tolkien, J. R. R. *Tree and Leaf*. London: Unwin, 1964.

Wolff, Robert Lee. *The Golden Key: A Study of the Fiction of George MacDonald*. New Haven: Yale University P, 1961.

Chapter Ten

George MacDonald in the Creative Writing Classroom: "The Wise Woman as a Possible Model"

Thom Satterlee

In the United States, over four hundred colleges and universities offer either a major or minor in creative writing to their undergraduate students (Fenza). As part of their degree completion, students take courses in which they write original works, often aided by professional models chosen by their instructors. If we examine the textbooks published to support these classes, we will find a variety of possible models. Most textbooks marketed for fiction writing classes, for instance, will include both classic and contemporary writers, some from the United States and some from around the world. The author of one such textbook states her commitment to variety plainly:

> I have tried to assemble a collection of stories, international in scope, that represent a wide variety of subject matter, theme, literary technique, and style, and that, at the same time, serve to illustrate the development of short fiction—its continuity, durability, and tradition—from its identifiable beginnings in the early years of the nineteenth century to the present.
> (Pickering vii).

Despite this stated desire for variety, however, almost all fiction writing textbooks (including the above) exclude a form of fiction that many students would be familiar with and might benefit from. I am referring to children's stories, by which I mean fiction whether realistic or fantastic written for children, though the author might well have had adults in mind as a secondary audience. Except for the occasional inclusion of a Hans Christian Andersen story, this type of fiction is wholly absent from the store of models made available through textbooks to instructors of fiction writing classes. I have begun to wonder why this is and whether there might be a case for making children's stories a regular part of a fiction writing class.

I believe that two assumptions underlie the choice to exclude children's stories. Firstly, stories written for adults appear to be more complex both in thought and linguistic range. University instructors wanting to challenge their students naturally select models that they believe demonstrate such complexities. Given the fact that creative writing is a relatively new addition to the university curriculum, writing instructors might feel a certain level of "status anxiety," too, and wish to associate themselves and their classes with only the more approved and serious works of literature. Secondly, children's stories may be seen, both by instructors and by the authors of fiction writing textbooks, as too message driven. Since contemporary tastes among writers and readers of serious literature are undeniably set against didacticism, it seems only reasonable for instructors to choose models that agree with the dominant aesthetic.

Taken together, these two perceived problems (simplicity and didacticism) create a barrier for instructors who might want to include children's stories in a university-level creative writing classroom. The loss in terms of variety to the curriculum is, I think, no small matter. Students beginning to concentrate on the craft of writing benefit from models that move them to emulation, and not all students will be moved by works written for adults. Given the fact, too, that most students at the undergraduate level will not go on to become professional writers, the tendency toward a monolithic curriculum seems unwarranted. Why not explore creative writing from a broader perspective if for most students the experience will be simply that, an exploration?

In the past I have used a short tale from Hans Christian Andersen with undergraduates in my Fiction Writing class. The story I chose, "Big Claus and Little Claus," was neither simple nor particularly didactic. By including it among the stories we read I was able to vary my offerings without necessarily disturbing the assumptions I share with other instructors of creative writing-- namely that good literature should be complex and should not impose the writer's views in a dogmatic fashion. Now, however, I am considering a children's story that, at least on its surface, violates both of these treasured standards. In the following I wish to examine the fairy tale "A Wise Woman" by the 19th-century Scottish writer George MacDonald. Could it, I am asking myself and fellow instructors, be a helpful model for students of creative writing?

MacDonald's story concerns two girls, one a princess and one the daughter of a shepherd. Although their backgrounds differ greatly, both were raised by indulgent parents and have become, by the moment of the story's main action, unmitigated brats. To their rescue comes a mysterious character with magical powers known to readers as the Wise Woman. Her desire is to help each become "good and lovely" (80). It would not be incorrect to state the story's theme as moral reformation, but it would be misleading to leave it at that. It would be misleading because of the implied word "simply" in front of the words "moral reformation." In fact, this story bears genuine witness to the struggles involved in becoming a good person and explores the roots of selfishness, anger, and conceit. True, the main characters in this story may be children, and the intended audience may be children, but adults can easily see themselves in the princess or the shepherd's daughter.

Both Rosamond (the princess) and Agnes (the shepherd's daughter) underestimate the difficulty of improving their characters. After a brief experience of suffering, Rosamond believes that "her soul had grown larger of a sudden, and she had left the days of her childishness and naughtiness far behind her" (23) only to discover that the slightest change in her circumstances provoked angry outbursts. Similarly, Agnes is too quick to consider herself permanently improved and must be told by the Wise Woman that "[she] must not consider herself cured" (52) after a short period of good behavior. The fact that the story ends with only one of the children having made positive progress, while the other has actually worsened, underscores the complexity of the story's theme. In fact, as I read the story I was often reminded of the adult struggles of a Saint Paul or Saint Augustine, especially when Rosamond, devastated by her failure to improve herself, declares, "I am made horrid, and I shall be horrid, and I hate myself, and yet I can't help being myself" (92).

In terms of subject matter, then, I do not consider "The Wise Woman" to be too simple. Personally, I am also impressed by its linguistic complexity and could easily imagine a fruitful class period spent anaylzing MacDonald's writing style. Those familiar with MacDonald may be surprised to hear praise for this writer's style, which C.S. Lewis described as "undistinguished, at times fumbling....[with] an old Scotch weakness for florid ornament" (ix). How ever much these qualities appear in other works by MacDonald, in "The Wise Woman" they are nearly absent, and in their place one finds many wonderfully sophisticated pieces of language. I would argue that the following, for instance, does not suffer from wordiness, though it might appear to at first:

> As she grew up, everybody about her did his best to convince her that she was a Somebody; and the girl herself was so easily persuaded of it that she forgot that anybody had even told her so, and took it for a fundamental, innate, primary, first-born, self-evident and incontrovertible idea and principle that *she was a Somebody.*
> (3)

This long sentence (not nearly the longest in the story, which includes two page-long sentences) is well balanced, breaking down into three main parts: "everybody did his best to convince her...," "the girl herself was so easily persuaded..." and "[she] took it for a fundamental...principle." The piling up of six adjectives before the noun "idea" and the use of a seemingly unnecessary synonym for "idea" convey a tone of mock-seriousness and establish the narrator's attitude towards the conceitedness that comes from thinking of oneself as a Somebody.

The story is also rich in figurative language, imagery, and lyrical phrasings. As an instructor of creative writing, I would be happy to hold up any of these as examples of strong imaginative writing:

> About the heath, on every side, lay the forest, looking in the moonlight like a cloud; and above the forest, like the shaven crown of a monk, rose the bare moor. (18-19)

> [The Wise Woman] set her down on the heath...[and] disappeared around the corner of the cottage, leaving the princess alone with the moon--two white faces in the cone of night. (19)

> His head struck on the boat as he fell, and he sank at once to the bottom, where he lay looking up at her with white face and open eyes. (86)

> She dreamed that she was the old cold woman up in the sky, with no home and no friends, and no nothing at all, not even a picket; wandering, wandering forever over a desert of blue sand, never to get to anywhere, and never to lie down or die. (24)

In "The Wise Woman," simplicity turns out not to be a real problem. MacDonald demonstrates sophistication both in terms of idea and expression and does so, I think, admirably. It is more difficult for me to justify the story's didacticism, however. After multiple readings I find the narrator a thin disguise for the author, whose opinions, even though I may agree with them, frequently interrupt the story. Moral pronouncements abound, and one hardly doubts that as readers we are meant to learn something. Most instructors of creative writing--themselves writers and readers of contemporary, non-didactic literature--will cringe at the following:

> For when people *will* be naughty, they have to be frightened, and they are not expected to like it. (15)

> [T]here are people—however unlikely it may seem--who object to doing a thing for no other reason than that it is required of them. (28)

> [T]he least atom of conceit is a thing to be ashamed of. (41)

> Vanity, which is a form of self-conceit, has repeatedly shown itself as the

George MacDonald in the Creative Writing Classroom: "The Wise Woman as a Possible Model"

deepest feeling in the heart of a horrible murderess. (43)

And our dislike for this sort of explicit teaching goes beyond mere taste. It isn't simply that as individuals we resist being told what to do and grow impatient at sermons; rather, on grounds of craft--on what makes a story work well--we prefer more subtle approaches to the matter of theme. In my entry-level course in creative writing, for instance, I assign this excerpt taken from the first chapter of my students' textbook:

> Although any character in a play or story, any speaker in a poem, is a partial revelation of the writer, the intention to reveal one's self or sell one's views is not a necessary or useful approach to the art....The conscious point of trying to make a point—of sending a message—can block the flow and distort the final shape of any literary work.
> (Jason and Lefcowitz 9)

These authors state what I believe most creative writing instructors take for granted--that good literature, though it may teach us something about ourselves, does so with a light hand, inviting rather than imploring readers to reconsider their lives. The overt lessons in MacDonald's "The Wise Woman" (which extend beyond the examples above and include moments when the narrator directly judges his characters) might be seen to undermine this fundamental and perhaps wise prohibition on didacticism. But do they?

Actually, I think assigning this story as a model would provide a rare opportunity to explore assumptions behind contemporary writing and open up discussion about the history of creative writing. Why were MacDonald's fairy stories popular with his 19th-century readers? Why should there be less tolerance for didacticism today? What have we lost by preferring a more subtle approach to storytelling? Students, I believe, quickly understand and sympathize with John Gardner's dictum that a story should be "an uninterrupted dream" and see that standard met in the works of the contemporary writers represented on their course syllabi. A story like MacDonald's would have the advantage of letting students question--once they first understand them--the assumptions behind the discipline they are studying.

The apparent disadvantage of didacticism in this story could be turned to other useful purposes. Along with the aesthetic questions "The Wise Woman" raises, it also offers intriguing possibilities for writing assignments. If a class agrees that the narrator's tendency to state moral truths and to pass judgment on his characters *is* a weakness of the story, what might the story look like with those passages removed? Students could be asked to revise passages by omitting any of the "offending" material and supplying any necessary transitions. Alternatively, students could be asked to write a story after the fashion of

MacDonald—let the didacticisms rip!—and compare their versions to his and to one another's. Doing so would likely reveal certain techniques that aid in the writing of a didactic story, such as humor and a certain amount of reader distancing, both of which occur in "The Wise Woman."

Of course, I cannot say without first trying whether including "The Wise Woman" (or some comparable children's story) in a creative writing class would work well or backfire. My one experience using the Hans Christian Andersen story, however, did prove successful. My students and I marvelled at the wild imagination in that story and, I believe, felt as inspired to write after reading it as we did after reading a variety of adult stories. Next semester, I hope to increase that variety by including MacDonald's fine story.

Works Cited

Fenza, David. "About AWP: The Growth of Creative Writing Programs." *AWP Website*. 28 Aug. 2007. <http://www.awpwriter.org/aboutawp/index.htm>.

Jason Philip K., and Allan B. Lefcowitz. *Creative Writer's Handbook*. Upper Saddle, NJ: Prentice Hall, 2005.

MacDonald, George. *The Wise Woman and Other Fantasy Stories*. Grand Rapids, MI: Eerdmans, 1980.

Pickering, James H. *Fiction 100: An Anthology of Short Fiction*. Upper Saddle, NJ: Prentice Hall, 2007.

CHAPTER ELEVEN

STORY AND THE CHILD READER TODAY

JUDITH ELKIN

Introduction

Even in the days of the Internet and technology beyond our wildest dreams, reading remains an essential skill and the book remains the medium of choice for millions of people for leisure reading, relaxation, and escapism. Earlier chapters have analysed the work of George MacDonald in depth. This chapter takes a more discursive approach, focusing on the child reader. It explores the joys and pleasures of reading and the particular role of story, fantasy and folk tale today. The place of MacDonald within a current reading context is explored.

The Power of Reading

A number of eloquent writers have considered why reading is important to them. In the compelling *Read For Your Life: Literature As a Life Support System*, Gold (1990) proposes that reading is a part of human survival:

> Reading is not necessary to our survival, if by survival we mean eating and staying warm. It is necessary to our larger survival, however, to an enriched, aware life in which we exercise some measure of control over our well-being, our creativity and our connection to everything around us (100)... When we practice reading as an art and a discipline, we are not wasting time and being frivolous and irresponsible... When we still the outside world and turn to our inner minds, we are exercising our imagination, and getting in touch with our feelings, increasing our information, coping with the world through simulated situations. We come back from reading refreshed, restored, recharged. (34)

Similarly, in his thought-provoking, *A History of Reading*, Manguel (1996) explores the joy of reading: "We read to understand, or to begin to understand...

Reading, almost as much as breathing, is our essential function." (7) He cites Kafka's belief that books should:

> bite and sting us. If the book we are reading doesn't shake us awake like a blow on the skull, why bother reading it in the first place? What we need are books that hit us like a painful misfortune, like the death of someone we loved more than we love ourselves, that make us feel as though we had been banished to the woods, far from any human presence, like a suicide. A book must be the axe for the frozen sea within us. (93)

Aidan Chambers (1986) talks about 'transformational' writing:

> literature which, if read creatively, reader and author making the story together, has the effect of transforming us as readers and as people…literary reading is the single most important cultural and educational activity we all – adults and children – engage in. Unless you find yourself in books you have a hard time finding anybody else (15-16) … transforming books are multi-layered, multi-thematic, linguistically conscious, dense. (19)

Spufford (2002), in his inspirational *The Child That Books Built*, also talks about readings that acted like transformations:

> There were times when a particular book, like a seed crystal, dropped into our minds when they were exactly ready for it, like a supersaturated solution and suddenly we changed. Suddenly a thousand crystals of perception of our own formed, the original insight of the story ordering whole arrays of discoveries inside us, into winking accuracy…The dominant sensation of reading was excited delight… The books you read as a child brought you sights you hadn't seen for yourself, scents you hadn't smelled, sounds you hadn't heard. They introduced you to people you hadn't met, and helped you to sample ways of being that would never have occurred to you. (9-10)

Margaret Meek (1982) acknowledges the particular bond between reader and writer:

> …not all the electronic media in the world will replace what happens when a reader meets a writer. Reading is far more than the retrieval of information from a collection of printed records. It is the active encounter of one mind and one imagination with another. Talk happens; the words fly, remembered or not. Writing remains; we read at our own pace, which is the rate of our thinking. Real reading cannot be done without thought. As it is a kind of "inner speech", it is bound to have a marked effect on the growth of the mind of the reader. (10-11)

Meek (1991) emphasises the fact that early reading builds lifelong reading as part of a developmental process towards creating "expert readers" and "powerful literates":

> Good readers are more than just successful print-scanners and retrievers of information – they find in books the depth and breadth of human experience – readers are at home in the life of the mind; they live with ideas as well as events and facts; they understand a wide range of feelings by entering into those of other people…Literate adults make their reading work for them. They use books as tools, as sources of information and means of checking. They choose with confidence what they want or need to read. (33)

Novelist, P.D. James (1992) reminds us that we have what is arguably:

> the most beautiful, the most versatile and the richest language in the world…To enjoy reading, to love books, is to have a source of joy, satisfaction and pleasure throughout the whole of life from childhood to old age, and a sure shield against its inevitable disappointments and griefs. (1-2)

The Child Reader

Within the context of the value of reading viewed from an adult perspective, the place of reading in the life of the child is perhaps even more critical. Children live very much more pressurised lives than the child of 100 years ago. Personal safety and over protection can dominate the freedom of the child, at a time when they mature and consider themselves adults at a very early age. Media and technology dominate their waking hours; communication has become global rather than personal and face-to-face. Thus, time and space for reading and the escapism provided by reading become ever more valuable; the opportunity for the child to get in touch with his or her feelings becomes of paramount importance.

Spufford (2002) describes his mother's reaction to his reading as a child:

> I can always tell when you're reading somewhere in the house. There's a special silence, a '*reading* silence.'" I never heard it, this extra depth of hush that somehow travelled through walls and ceilings to announce that my seven-year-old self had become as absent as a present person can be. The silence went both ways. As my concentration on the story in my hands took hold, all sounds faded away…The silence that fell on the noises of people and traffic and dogs allowed an inner door to open to the book's data, its script of sound. (1)

Readers often talk about being "lost in a book", a feeling of being so engrossed in an activity that nothing else matters. Manguel (1996) recognizes this state as being: "buried in books, isolated from the world of facts and flesh, feeling superior to those unfamiliar with the words preserved between dusty covers." (296)

Novelist Anita Desai (2002), as a child in India was known in her family as a Lese Ratte or "reading rat", a bookworm. She remembers her own world receding, when she discovered Emile Brönte's *Wuthering Heights* at the age of nine:

> an old Delhi bungalow, its verandas and plastered walls and ceiling fans, its garden of papaya and guava trees full of shrieking parakeets, the gritty dust that settled on the pages of a book before one could turn them, all receded. What became real, dazzlingly real, through the power and magic of Emily Brönte's pen, were the Yorkshire moors, the storm-driven heath, the torments of its anguished inhabitants, who roamed therein in rain and sleet, crying out from the depths of their broken hearts and hearing only ghosts reply. (208)

The magic of reading and its ability to transport the child reader to unlimited new worlds is beautifully described through Bastiona Nalthazar Bux's passion for books in Michael Ende's *The Neverending Story* (1984):

> If you have never spent whole afternoons with burning ears and rumpled hair, forgetting the world around you over a book, forgetting cold and hunger – if you have never read secretly under the bedclothes with a flashlight, because your father or mother or some other well-meaning person has switched off the lamp on the plausible ground that it was time to sleep because you had to get up so early. If you have never wept bitter tears because a wonderful story has come to an end and you must take your leave of the characters with whom you have shared so many adventures, whom you have loved and admired, for whom you have hoped and feared, and without whose company life seems empty and meaningless – If such things have not been part of your experience, you probably won't understand what Bastian did next…Staring at the title of the book, he turned hot and cold, cold and hot. Here was just what he had dreamed of, what he had longed for ever since the passion for books had taken hold of him. A story that never ended! The book of books!! (10)

In the 21st century, it remains essential that children are offered every available stimulus and support, so that they do not miss out on the opportunity to become "powerful literates", to enjoy the sensations mentioned above, to have a real understanding of the many pleasures and passions that reading and enjoyment of books can bring.

Hooked On Books

The passionate reader, once hooked, will read eclectically and widely, devouring easy books, demanding books, chilling books, the classics, modern literature, struggling with the impossible. The challenge, then, to parents, grandparents, carers, teachers and librarians is to ensure access to the wealth of stimulating and exciting literature available, both current and historical literature. Perhaps, this is more critical in the twenty first century than ever before, not least because the competition for children's and young people's time is at such a premium.

It is worth revisiting Bettina Hurlimann (1967), writing in the 1960s, for her enduring view that:

> in this restless age of technology, when the emphasis is always on records of attainment and productivity, there is some danger of forgetting that a child does not require too much in the way of books...What he does need are the right books at the right time so that he may find in literature a true point of balance in an often disordered world. It is for us as parents or teachers, librarians or publishers, to recognize this need and to know how best, how most imaginatively, to fulfil it. (xviii)

Spufford (2002) relates how he was turned on to reading:

> When I caught the mumps, I couldn't read; when I went back to school, I could. The first page of *The Hobbit* was a thicket of symbols, to be decoded one at a time and joined hesitantly together...By the time I reached *The Hobbit's* last page, writing had softened, and lost the outlines of the printed alphabet, and become a transparent liquid, first viscous and sluggish, like a jelly of meaning, then ever thinner and more mobile, flowing faster and faster, until it reached me at the speed of thinking and I could not entirely distinguish the suggestions it was making from my own thoughts. I had undergone the acceleration into the writing word. (64-65)

> So the reading flowed, when I was six, with the yellow hardback copy of *The Hobbit* in my hands; and the pictures came. I went to the door of the hobbit hole with Bilbo as he let in more, and more, and more dwarves attracted by the sign Gandalf had scratched there in the glossy green paint. I jogged with him on his pony out of the Shire, away from the raspberry jam and crumpets, and towards dragons. (69)

Author Philip Pullman (2002) talks about "the silence of the written word – tentative, provisional, hesitant - private words, secret words communicating in silence with the private world of the reader."

Arts Council England (2003) is adamant about the importance of the role of reading in the twenty first century. Its recent review of children's literature, *From Looking Glass To Spyglass* recognizes:

> ...children's literature as the touchstone for a healthy and sustainable literary culture. Children's writers and illustrators reach readers at their most dependent and travel with them through to young adulthood and beyond...It affords the means by which children can dialogue with their futures, not only through the printed word, but also through children's literature's intimate connections with the visual arts and design, film and television, theatre and new technologies. Its value is private and public, cultural and artistic, and also social and economic. (3)

The OECD (Organisation for Economic Cooperation and Development) report, *Reading For Change* (2002) reinforces the importance of literacy in a global context:

Literacy is no longer considered an ability only acquired in childhood during the early years of schooling. Instead, it is viewed as an expanding set of knowledge, skills and strategies which individuals build on throughout life in various situations and through interaction with their peers and with the larger communities in which they participate. (24)

The OECD also acknowledges that reading literacy is a dynamic rather than a static concept that needs to parallel changes in society and culture:

> The reading literacy needed for individual growth, economic participation and citizenship 20 years ago were different from what is expected today...We live in a rapidly changing world, where both the number and types of written materials are increasing and where growing numbers of people are expected to use these materials in new and sometimes more complex ways. (16)

Story

Reading, as demonstrated above, is a wonderfully solitary and empowering occupation but sharing stories and reading together has inestimable value, too. Trelease (1982) emphasises the pleasure of shared reading with his own children:

> We have searched for wayward brothers and sisters, evaded wolves, lost friends and learned how to make new ones. We have laughed, cried, shaken with fright, and shivered with delight. And best of all, we did it together. Along the way we discovered something about the universality of human experience – that we, too, have many of the hopes and fears of the people we read about. The cost of such a wondrous experience is well within your means...It costs you time and

interest, if you are willing to invest both, you can pick up a book, turn to a child, and begin today. I promise you, you will never want the experience to end. (22)

Meek (1991) reminds us that story is fundamental to all societies and storytelling is part of our heritage. She sees storytelling as a universal habit, a part of our common humanity:

> All cultures have some form of narrative. Stories are part of our conversation, our recollections, our plans, our hopes, our fears. Young and old, we all tell stories as soon as we begin to explain or describe events and actions, feelings and motives. (103)

> ...in human remembering the past stays alive, so story-telling not only supplies children with memories they cannot yet have, it also gives them 'virtual' memory, the idea of remembering what they have heard others tell...Story-telling lies at the back of all literacy, powerful in its effect and distinguished by its cultural differences. (65)

Meek (1982) reminds us that children learn stories in the playground:

> ...stories that are secrets, narrative initiation rites of the new tribe, that seem, but only seem, to disappear. This is the time to discover storying as gossip and scandal, to overturn the established mode of orderly telling, to introduce incoherence and chaos, crisis and social drama. (9)

Chambers (1982) echoes this, seeing story as the fundamental grammar of all thought and of all communication:

> By telling ourselves what happened, to whom, and why we not only discover ourselves and the world, we change and create ourselves and the world too...Story is not only about the who and the what and the why. It is not only about character, action and motivation...It is quite as importantly about the how. As our finest critical readers have so often shown, how a story is made tells us quite as much about the world as a writer understands it as anything in the story's content. (15)

Story itself remains important; we continue to rely on story to sort out our world:

> we dream in narrative, daydream in narrative, remember, anticipate, hope, despair, believe, doubt, plan, revise, criticize, construct, gossip, learn, hate, and love by narrative. In order really to live, we make up stories about ourselves and others, about the personal as well as the social past and future. (Hardy,1977,13)

behind the news bulletin, the strip cartoon, the sports report. Ask a friend about his holiday, how he moved house, what happened to his car, wife, sweetheart, dog and the result will be narrative. We sort out our sense impressions into storying. (Meek, Warlow and Barton, 1977, 7-8)

Storyteller Grace Hallworth (1985) believes we cannot take steps in life or literature without narrating:

...of dreams, of love affairs, trials and tribulations of the wife, the husband, the child...science and technology uses the anecdotal method of storytelling. Sharing is central to strategies of encouraging international understanding and developing heightened sensitivities to other cultures, as well as our own culture...We need to build a bridge between the culture of literature and the culture of life...in many cultures, grandmothers provide this source...All children should have their horizons given psychological and physical breadth – exploration and habitation of worlds in space. It is part of the cultural mosaic from which we gain; folklore shows how we are the same and uniquely different; it reflects the universal human predicament...if you take a person's folklore and dialect, you begin to enter into/to see another culture.

Fantasy and Fairy Tale

So, how do fantasy and fairy tale fit into the broader literary canon, in terms of accessibility and readability for children and young people in today's world?

In his seminal work, *The Uses of Enchantment* (1976), Bruno Bettelheim suggests that:

Fairy tales reassure because they demonstrate that others have the same kind of fantasies; children possess an inner world of fantasy which is irrational, subjective, sensual, violent and often frightening. Fairy tales can bring order to the child's inner life by offering symbolic solutions to his difficulties...they both reflect the child's inner life and convey a sense of order.

While it entertains the child, the fairy tale enlightens him about himself, and fosters his personality development...Fairy tales are unique, not only as a form of literature, but as works as art which are fully comprehensible to the child, as no other form of art is. As with all great art, the fairy tale's deepest meaning will be different for each person, and different for the same person at various moments in his life. (12)

...these tales, in a much deeper way than any other reading material, start where the child really is in his psychological and emotional being. They speak about his severe inner pressures in a way that the child unconsciously understands and – without belittling the most serious inner struggles which growing up entails – offer examples of both temporary and permanent solutions to pressing difficulties…The fairy tale…confronts the child squarely with the basic human predicaments. (56)

Meek (1982) emphasizes, in particular, the global value of fairy tales which:

> initiate us and our children into the wisdom of not only our local culture – important though that is – but also into a universal culture unity of motifs, forms and characters. They are our most helpful means of becoming truly multicultural, at home in the wider world as well as in a particular corner of it. (8)

Fantasy means literally 'a making visible'. All fantasy is that:

> whether it is a shape and substance given to things not actually present, to the stuff of secret dreams, or to things which never were or could be. And certainly, for writers and readers – adult or child – who are concerned with the *art* of fantasy, the world is still as broad as all imagination. (Curry, 1980, 83)

Fantasy is closely related to the traditional fairy story. The birth of fantasy writing in Britain coincided with the 19th century revival of interest in the orally transmitted fairy tale. George MacDonald, a leading contributor to this revival, was much influenced by Hans Andersen, the author of over 150 Fairy Stories and other tales, either of his own invention or based on folk themes. This era, of the late nineteenth century, has often been referred to as the Golden Age of Fantasy. George MacDonald clearly belongs here, alongside Charles Kingsley, Lewis Carroll and Oscar Wilde.

MacDonald was adamant about the importance of abiding by the laws of fantasy once their basis had been established. This approach or concept can be seen as the basic tenet of good fantasy writing ever since and a significant early influence on writers of the genre. It is also the inter-connection between realism and fantasy and focus on relationships set in a realistic context, that make MacDonald's stories particularly influential on later writers but also pertinent to whole generations of children up to the present time. Writers from Edith Nesbit, C.S Lewis, Enid Blyton and many others were much influenced by MacDonald's work, and owe a huge debt of gratitude to him.

A recent contribution to the debate on applying critical standards to reading habits of children, has taken fantasy as its theme. (Moody and Horrocks, 2005). The essays in this collection include a number of references to MacDonald, in terms of his lasting influence as a very early proponent of fantasy writing for children and as an influence on many later writers of the genre. Particular note is given to MacDonald's attention to detail, the quality of his writing and in particular to his commitment to the "imaginary wholeness" (200) of the fantasy worlds he created.

A second Golden Age of Fantasy in the United Kingdom can be viewed as the 1950's, 1960's and 1970's, when fantasy writing for children again flourished, much of it reflecting the heritage of MacDonald, in particular combining the realities of the social context with fantasy.

The third Golden Age of Fantasy is with us now, with fantasy writing more popular than ever. Although, in reality, it can be seen that fantasy writing for children has never really faded away in UK but, rather, has remained a genre that has attracted some of the best children's authors, in terms of originality, imagination and the superb quality of their writing, since the 1960's. Many of the best UK writers write within the broad category of fantasy; fascinatingly, this is untrue, with a few notable exceptions, of American writing, but that discussion is beyond the scope of this chapter.

Key authors of the 1950's and 1960's, many of them writing over decades included: C.S. Lewis and the Narnia series (recently rejuvenated through film); J.R.R. Tolkien with his *Lord of The Rings* trilogy (again powerfully presented in film); Philippa Pearce with *Tom's Midnight Garden*; Alan Garner, with early titles such as *The Weirdstone of Brisingamen* and the later, powerful *Red Shift;* Diana Wynne Jones, with her Chrestomanci stories.

Over the last decade, J.K. Rowling's *Harry Potter* series, which blend folk tale, myth and fantasy with traditional school stories, have dominated the scene. The stories (and films) have grabbed the interests and passions of millions of children around the world, but, in something of a throwback to the MacDonald tradition, have captured the imagination of adults, too. Their quality, pace and sheer readability has motivated even less able readers to read the unfashionably long stories and has found children around the world fighting to read the stories in English, because they couldn't wait for the books to be translated into their own languages. They have become a powerful phenomenon and have had the great benefit of turning many children and young people back to reading or enjoying the excitement of reading for the first time.

The Potter books have been a particular phenomenon, but other authors, for example, Philip Pullman with *His Dark Materials* trilogy, a much darker, possibly more skilled series, has similarly had a global reach with committed readers, again demonstrating the power of story. Other contemporary authors, such as Melvyn Burgess, David Arnold, and Peter Dickinson, with stories such as *Eva,* are stretching young minds to ever more challenging ideas.

MacDonald Today

Returning to MacDonald, what of his impact on today's young readers? Does he still have an appeal to the reader today? Does he still have the power to bond with today's reader? Where does MacDonald's work sit alongside others children's classics? Classics suggest an excellence surviving from a past age; a book whose popularity has survived the age in which it was written:

> such a book does not simply endure like a fossil in a glass cage, but is constantly re-made and improvised upon so that its qualities and its appeal are transformed and revealed to new generations of readers. (Watson, 1994, 32)
>
> A characteristic of the classic children's story is its capacity to offer from within itself new meanings and fresh emphases while retaining its original integrity. (34)

Rachel Johnson (2004) in her research on George MacDonald, carried out a number of in-depth interviews with children, in order to assess the timelessness, the lasting quality and relevance of some of MacDonald's work, exploring the "intrinsic value" of fairy tales to engender thought on moral issues.

The discussion with seven year old Lizzie, focused on *The Princess and the Goblin*, although she was already familiar with, and had clearly enjoyed *The Light Princess and Other Stories*. Even at seven, Lizzie was able to distinguish and appreciate what she called: "a real side and a magical side" of the story, as well as the good and the bad and assessed the relevance of the story to her: "the magic needs to make all the difference to a story to be acceptable in a story." Perceptively, Lizzie also acknowledges that "it was a fairy tale...because it makes you think." How perceptive, but also how eminently valuable in today's world, stories that stretch the imagination of the child and make them think; clearly timeless!

12 year old David was introduced to *The Light Princess and other Fairy Tales*. He was a voracious and thoughtful reader with a preference for fantasy. However, he had not met MacDonald before, so his reactions were fresh. David observed that the story was less stereotyped than traditional tales, that the characters were less clear cut and simple and that "it was more like a real life scenario." David was aware that the story could be read at a variety of levels, the reader taking whatever they wanted from the story; again a test for an enduring classic.

This maybe is the real test of any good story. MacDonald (1890) himself felt that: "Everyone who feels the story, will read its meaning after his own nature and development."

Johnson's research shows clearly that the quality of writing, the quality of story and character and dealing with fundamental values makes MacDonald's work as relevant today as when they were first written, although the social context has changed out of all recognition. Perhaps, children have never stopped enjoying folktales, fairy tales and fantasy and the excellent ones will survive.

As Townsend (1971) wrote:

Children's Literature has wild blood in it; its ancestry lies partly in the long ages of storytelling. Myth, legend, fairy tale are alive in their own right, endlessly re-printed, endlessly fertile in their influence. (220)

How wonderful that children's literature still has wild blood in it and what an inheritance to leave to our children.

Works Cited

Arts Council England *From Looking Glass To Spyglass: A Consultation Paper On Children's Literature*. London: Arts Council England, 2003.

Bettelheim, B. *The Uses Of Enchantment: The Meaning And Importance Of Fairy Tales*. London: Thames and Hudson, 1976.

Butler, D. *Babies Need Books: Sharing The Joy Of Books With Children From Birth To Six*. Revised edition, London: The Bodley Head, 1998.

Byatt, A.S. In Van Riel, R. editor. *Reading The Future: a Place For Literature In Public Libraries*. A report of the seminar held in York 2 and 3 March 1992, organised by the Arts Council of Great Britain in association with the Library Association and the Regional Arts Boards of England,1992.

Chambers, A. *The Reluctant Reader*. Oxford: Pergamon, 1969.

—. *Booktalk: Occasional Writing On Literature And Children*. London: The Bodley Head, 1985.

—. The Child's Changing Story. In *Story in The Child's Changing World: Papers And Proceedings Of The 18th Congress Of The International Board On Books For Young People*, Churchill College, Cambridge, 1982.

Chambers, N. editor *The Signal Approach To Children's Books: A Collection*. London: Kestrel, 1980.

Curry, Jane. On The Elvish Craft. In *The Signal Approach To Children's Books: A Collection*, edited by Nancy Chambers. London: Kestrel Books, 1980.

Desai, A. A Reading Rat On the Moors. In *Soho Square III*, ed. Alberto Manguel, London: 1990.

Ende, M. *The Neverending Story*, tr. Ralph Manheim. London: Penguin Books, 1984.

Fox,G., et al *Writers, Critics And Children*. London: Heinemann Educational Press, 1976.

Gold, Joseph *Read For Your Life: Literature As A Life Support System*. Ontario: Fitzhenry & Whiteside, 1990.

Hallworth, G. speaking publicly at UNESCO/IFLA conference: The Library, a centre for promoting international understanding, Salamanca, Spain, June, 1985. unpublished.

Hardy, B. Narrative As A Primary Act Of Mind. In Meek, M., Warlow, A., Barton, G. *The Cool Web: The Pattern Of Children's Reading*. London: The Bodley Head, 1977.

Hurlimann, B. *Three Centuries Of Children's Books in Europe*, translated and edited by B. Alderson. London: Oxford University Press, 1967.

James, P.D. In Van Riel, R. ed. *Reading the Future: a Place For Literature In Public Libraries*. A report of the seminar held in York 2 and 3 March 1992, organised by the Arts Council of Great Britain in association with the Library Association and the Regional Arts Boards of England, 1992.

Johnson, Rachel 'The Magic Makes All the Difference: George MacDonald's Fairy Tales, A Child's Eye View.' In *Inklings Forever*: Volume IV. A Collection of Essays Presented at the Fourth Frances White Ewbank Colloquium on C.S. Lewis and Friends. Taylor University March 12-14, 2004. Upland, Indiana, 2004.

MacDonald, George 'The Fantastic Imagination' in *A Dish Of Orts*. London: Sampson Low, Marston & Co. , 1890. Whitethorn, CA: Johannesen, 1996, 351,

Manguel, A. *A History Of Reading*. London: Viking, 1996.

Meek, M. *Learning To Read*. London: The Bodley Head, 1982.

—. The Role Of Story In The Child's Changing World. In *Story In The Child's Changing World: papers and proceedings of the 18th Congress of the International Board on Books for Young People,* Churchill College, Cambridge, 1982.

—. *On Being Literate*. London: The Bodley Head., 1991.

—. Warlow, A., Barton, G. *The Cool Web: The Pattern Of Children's Reading*. London: The Bodley Head, 1977.

Moody, Nickianne and Horrocks, Clare *Children's Fantasy Fiction: Debates For The Twenty First Century*. Liverpool: Association for Research in Popular Fiction and Liverpool John Moores University, 2005.

Organisation for Economic Cooperation and Development *Reading For Change: Performance And Engagement Across Countries, results from PISA 2000*. Paris: OECD, 2002.

Pullman, P. Accepting the Eleanor Farjeon Award. London: September 2002.

Spufford, F. *The Child That Books Built: A Memoir Of Childhood And Reading*. London: Faber, 2002.

—. Pillow Talk: Are You Snuggled Up? *The Guardian,* G2, 13.03.02, 2002.

Townsend, J.R. *Written For Children: An Outline Of English-Language Children's Literature*. 5th edition, 25th anniversary edition. London: The Bodley Head, 1990.

Trelease, J. *The Read Aloud Handbook,* London: Penguin, 1982.

Watson, Victor) What Makes a Children's Classic? In *The Best of Books For Keeps: Highlights From The Leading Children's Book Magazine,* edited by Chris Powling. London: The Bodley Head, 1994.

CONTRIBUTORS

Dr. Yuko Ashitagawa teaches English in Japan. She completed her PhD thesis "Reading and Writing the Primitive: Written Oralities and Fairy-Tale Studies" at the University of Reading in 2005. Her interests in children's literature include fantasy literature and critical theory. One of her recent publications is "On the Reading of Fairy Tales" *Journal of the Japan Society for Children's Literature in English* No. 50, February 2005.

Dr. William (Bill) Gray, is Reader in Literary History and Hermeneutics at the University of Chichester. He studied literature, philosophy and theology at the universities of Oxford, Edinburgh and Princeton, and has published in all these areas. In addition to his books *C.S. Lewis* (Northcote, 1998) and *Robert Louis Stevenson: A Literary Life* (Palgrave Macmillan, 2004), he has published chapters and articles on Goethe, Novalis, MacDonald, Stevenson, Lewis and Philip Pullman. His third year course "Other Worlds: Fantasy Literature for Children of All Ages" explores the origins of fantasy literature in German Romanticism, and its development into later examples of the genre, from MacDonald to Pullman. Currently Bill is working on a book for Palgrave Macmillan with the working title *Fantasy Fiction from E.T.A. Hoffmann to Philip Pullman*.

Professor Judith Elkin is Deputy Vice Chancellor at the University of Worcester; previously she was Dean of the Faculty of Computing, Information and English at UCE, Birmingham and Head of Children's Library Services in Birmingham. Judith Elkin is currently the Chair of the Board of the MLA West Midlands: Museums, Libraries and Archives Council and serves on a number of Boards i.e. West Midlands Higher Education Association Management Group and the Wolfson/CURL selection panel. Judith has a national and international reputation in the world of libraries and information science, especially in the fields of children's literature and literacy, reader development and multicultural literature and libraries. She has published widely in the fields of library and information studies, specialising in the study of literacy, reader development and multi-cultural children's literature. Publications include; *Focus on the Child: libraries, literacy and learning* (Library Association 1996), a critical analysis of library services to young people in the UK; *A Place for Children:*

public libraries as a major force in children's reading (Facet 2000); *Reading and reader development; the pleasure of reading* (Facet 2003); and a chapter in Charles Butler's *Teaching Children's Fiction* (Palgrave Macmillan 2006).

Dr. Larry E. Fink is Professor of English at Hardin-Simmons University in Abilene, Texas, where he has taught since 1988. His MA thesis (Hardin-Simmons University) was on C. S. Lewis, and his PhD dissertation (Texas A&M University) was on Milton. He regularly teaches classes on Milton, the English novel, C. S. Lewis, and the modern fantasy novel. Dr. Fink and Rolland Hein published the pictorial biography, *George MacDonald: Images of His World*, (Pasture Spring Press 2004). He is an active member of the Conference on Christianity & Literature, the C. S. Lewis & Inklings Society, and the George MacDonald Society. He regularly reads papers at meetings of these groups. Larry and his wife Cathy married in 1973 and have three grown children: Rachel, Stephen, and Mary.

Rachel Johnson is a Librarian at the University of Worcester UK. Her current work includes the establishment of Research Collections in the area of Children's Literature and supporting staff and students within the Institute of Education. She is studying part time for a PhD. With the Department of Arts, Humanities and Social Sciences. She completed her Masters in Education (Literacy and Children's Literature) from the University of Worcester in 2001. Her current research interests focus on the work of George MacDonald (1823 - 1905), and G. A. Henty (1832 - 1902), writer of historical adventure stories for boys.

Prof. Roderick McGillis is a Professor of English at the University of Calgary. He has published widely, including the edited collections *For the childlike: George MacDonald's fantasies for children* (Scarecrow Press 1992) and *Voices of the other: children's literature and the postcolonial context* (Garland 2000). In 2007 Routledge will publish a book on the Gothic and children's literature which he edited with Anna Jackson and Karen Coats. He is also currently editing a volume of essays on George MacDonald.

Prof. Maria Nikolajeva is a Professor of comparative literature at Stockholm University. She is the author and editor of several books, among them *Children's Literature Comes of Age: Toward the New Aesthetic* (Garland 1996); *How Picturebooks Work*, co-authored with Carole Scott (Garland 2001); *From Mythic to Linear: Time in Children's Literature* (Scarecrow

Press 2002); *The Rhetoric of Character in Children's Literature* (Scarecrow Press 2002), and *Aesthetic Approaches to Children's Literature* (Scarecrow Press 2005). From 1993-97 she was the President of the International Research Society for Children's Literature, and has served twice on Children's Literature Association international committee. She was also one of the senior editors for *The Oxford Encyclopaedia of Children's Literature* (Oxford 2006) and received the International Grimm Award in 2005.

Prof. David L. Neuhouser, Ph.D. Florida State University, is Professor Emeritus of Mathematics at Taylor University in the United States. He has served as Mathematics Department Chair, Director of the Honors Program, and is currently Director of the Center for the Study of C. S. Lewis & Friends. He is the recipient of several awards for teaching and for writing and has been a speaker at numerous conferences in the U.S. and in the U.K. In addition to many articles and reviews, he compiled the anthology, *George MacDonald: Selections From His Greatest Works* (Johannesen 1990) and is the author of *Open to Reason* (Taylor University Press 2001). He is the book reviewer for the George MacDonald quarterly publication, *Wingfold*.

Thom Satterlee is Director of Programs at the Center for the Study of C.S. Lewis and Friends at Taylor University in Upland, Indiana, as well as an associate professor of English at the same institution. His main area of teaching is creative writing. He earned his degrees from Houghton College (B.A. Philosophy), State University of New York, College at Brockport (M.A. English Literature/Creative Writing), and the University of Arkansas (M.F.A. Creative Writing/Literary Translation). His publications include a volume of original poems, a collection of poems translated from the Danish, and an edited collection of world literature on the sport of soccer.

Prof. Elmar Schenkel taught at the universities of Tübingen, Freiburg and at Amherst/Massachusetts and was visiting professor at Russian universities. Since 1993 he has been Chair of English Literature at the University of Leipzig. His research areas include science/literature, children's literature and travel writing. He has published books on British poetry, the Romantic essay, J.C. Powys, Tolkien, and H.G.Wells as well as travelogues on Japan, USA, and India; poetry and stories. His articles include work on MacDonald, Chesterton, Borges, Owen Barfield and others. His latest books include essays on eccentric and visionary scientists (*Die elektrische Himmelsleiter*) and a Russian travel book (*Das sibirische Pendel*). Elmar has also translated the poetry of Ted Hughes, Basil Bunting and Iain Crichton Smith and is on the editorial board of *Inklings Yearbook*.

Prof. Jean Webb is Professor of International Children's Literature at the University of Worcester, where she is Director of the International Centre for Research in Children's Literature, Literacy and Creativity. Her research interests include children's literature from an international perspective, 19th and 20th century children's literature, and Irish Literature, since her PhD was on the drama of Sean O'Casey. Recent publications include: *Introducing Children's Literature: Romanticism to Postmodernism* co-authored with Deborah Cogan Thacker (Routledge 2002); editor *The Sunny Side Of Darkness: Children's Literature in Totalitarian and Post-Totalitarian Eastern Europe* (University of Tallinn 2005); 'Genre and Convention' in Butler C. (ed), *Teaching Children's Literature (*Palgrave MacMillan 2006); 'Beyond the Knowing: The Frontier of the Real and the Imaginary in David Almond's *Skellig* and *The Fire-Eaters'* in *Towards or Back to Human Values. Spiritual and Moral Dimensions of Contemporary Fantasy* edited by Justyna Deszcz-Tryhubczak and Marek Oziewicz. (Cambridge Scholars Press, 2006).